A NATURE LOVER'S ALMANAC

A NATURE LOVER'S ALMANAC

KINKY BUGS
STEALTHY CRITTERS
PROSPEROUS PLANTS
& CELESTIAL WONDERS

Diane Olson

Illustrated by **Adele Flail**

GIBBS SMITH
TO ENRICH AND INSPIRE HUMANKIND

First Edition
16 15 14 13 12   5 4 3 2 1

Published by
Gibbs Smith
P.O. Box 667
Layton, Utah 84041

1.800.835.4993 orders
www.gibbs-smith.com

Designed by Kurt Wahlner
Printed and bound in Hong Kong

Gibbs Smith books are printed on paper produced from
sustainable PEFC-certified forest/controlled wood source.
Learn more at www.pefc.org.

Library of Congress Cataloging-in-Publication Data

Olson, Diane.
A nature lover's almanac : kinky bugs, stealthy critters,
prosperous plants & celestial wonders / Diane Olson ; illustrated
by Adele Flail. — 1st ed.
      p. cm.
Based on the "Urban almanac" column in Salt Lake City's Catalyst
magazine.
ISBN 978-1-4236-2224-6
1. Natural history—Miscellanea. 2. Nature—Miscellanea.
3. Gardening—Miscellanea. 4. Almanacs. I. Catalyst magazine.
II. Title.
QH45.5.O57 2012
578—dc23
                              2011046574

PROLOGUE

It's easy to become disconnected from the natural world, especially for those of us who live and work in cities. We work inside hermetically sealed buildings; we commute; we go home and work some more. And we despair that we don't have the time, the money, or whatever it is we think we need more of before we can get out and engage with nature.

But we don't have to go into the wilderness to find nature. It's everywhere.

Bring home a potted plant and a whole new ecosystem springs into action around it. Dig a hole, fill it with water and *voila,* primordial soup. For that matter, our bodies are bustling with tiny creatures that feed off our secretions, skin and hair.

If you want to connect with the natural world, all you have to do is pay attention. Nothing is too small to be unimportant—or uninteresting.

January 1   January takes its name from Janus, the two-faced God who guards the passage between past and future. In days gone by, many Native American tribes kept track of the seasons by the recurring full moon. This was the month of the Full Wolf Moon or Full Old Moon.

January 2

HINTS
OF AN
APPROACHING

SNOW STORM

- High, thick cirrostratus clouds
- A halo around the sun or moon
- A sudden drop in the cloud ceiling
- Smoke from chimneys barely rises, due to low pressure

January 3

Tonight and tomorrow night, look to the north for the **Quadrantid meteor shower**, visible in the Northern Hemisphere, radiating from near the constellation Boötes. The Quadrantid shower is one of the year's best, typically producing over 100 meteors per hour.

January 4

Earth reaches **perihelion**, its annual position closest to the sun today. During winter, the lower altitude of the sun means its light hits our hemisphere at an oblique angle, causing the atmosphere to dissipate the heat.

January 5

Feed the birds! Seeds make great fodder, but birds also need fatty foods, like suet cakes and peanut butter, during cold weather.

January 6

Magpies

Black-billed magpies are frequent and rowdy visitors to winter suet feeders. Omnivorous and resourceful, magpies forage for insects, berries, seeds and carrion; they pick ticks off horses, cows  and deer and routinely pilfer from predators and other birds. They often make food caches, into which they deposit fresh and regurgitated snacks. Magpies can find food by scent, which is unusual in the avian world, as most birds have limited sense of smell.

January 7

There's always plenty in the natural world to engage the senses, even in the midst of winter.

During the day, look for trees and shrubs with interesting forms, like weeping crabapple and cherry, sumac and corkscrew willow, or those with cool seedpods, like catalpa, red bud, honeylocust, sycamore and linden.

At night, look for planets (stars scintillate, while planets shine more steadily and appear disc-shaped) and constellations. Take a deep breath. What kind of firewood is burned in your area? Cedar? Maple? Oak? Pinion? Juniper? They all have distinctive aromas.

Day or night, pay attention to the feel of the earth beneath your feet and the air against your skin.

January 8

SKUNK!

You just might encounter a skunk in your rambles. Skunks stay active all winter, foraging for rodent nestlings, snails, fallen fruit and old vegetables, carrion and garbage. Don't worry—skunks typically give plenty of warning and generally are not trigger-happy. Before spraying, they do an elaborate warning dance, which, in the spotted skunk, includes a handstand. But if that doesn't do the trick, nipples leading from the anal glands pop out, adjust, and rotate like an anti-aircraft gun. If they're near enough, the attacker gets a jet right in the eyes; otherwise, an all-encompassing mist is exuded.

January 9

Though it seems they do, fruit flies do not spontaneously generate from ripening fruit; they can just smell it from a long way away. The fruit fly has 32 odor receptors on each antenna, and all are honed to sniff out its favorite food—yeast.

Female fruit flies both feed on fermenting fruit and lay their eggs in it—400 to 500 of them, in fact. They hatch in half a day, and the larvae feed for about four days before they pupate. Four days later, another generation of randy, red-eyed adults emerges ready to perpetuate the cycle.

Fruit fly courtship and mating are ceremonial and lengthy. The male must perform a five-step song-and-dance number to the female's liking (the re-dos can take hours) before he's allowed to transfer his sperm cells. That takes at least 30 minutes. The female then stores the sperm until she finds a suitable time and place to process it and lay her eggs.

Should you run out of slightly slimy fruit, worry not; fruit flies can sustain themselves on sink drain slime, moist crumbs, and even alcohol fumes. Seriously, though, to rid your kitchen of fruit flies, tape a sheet of paper into a funnel and put it into a jar baited with a few ounces of cider vinegar. They won't be able to resist.

January 10

Coywolves,

coyote/wolf hybrids, are flourishing in southeastern Canada and the northeastern U.S. One is even reputed to be living in New York City's Central Park. Larger than coyotes but smaller than wolves, they are strong enough to hunt deer and are able to coexist with humans. And unlike many interbred species, their offspring are fertile.

January 11

If you have a pond with over-wintering fish, make sure a section is always ice-free.

January 12

Unlike most insects, **earwigs** are good mothers. They keep their eggs warm and clean and vigorously protect them from predators. As the eggs hatch, the mother assists them, and the nymphs nest under her like baby birds. Mama earwigs even regurgitate food for their babies until they're able to hunt and forage on their own.

January 13

Noctilucent clouds are rare, lovely, blue-white tendrils, most often seen in the western sky half an hour to an hour after sunset. They form in the mesosphere, about 50 miles up, where it's very cold and dry, and are composed of tiny ice crystals.

January 14

Back in our more hirsute days, **goose bumps** served a function: contracting the tiny muscles at the base of each hair created a fluffy layer of insulation, helping to retain body heat.

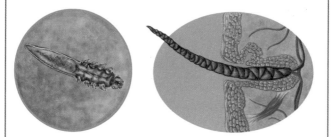

January 15

We all have **follicle mites** living on our faces, primarily in our eyelashes and eyebrows. They wander from hair to hair, feeding on skin cells, hormones, and oils, occasionally ducking inside a follicle opening for a quickie. After mating, the female lays her eggs inside a follicle or sebaceous gland. The larvae hatch in three to four days and take only a week to develop into adults. Fortunately, the follicle mite's digestive system is so efficient that it has no excretory orifice.

January 16

A chameleon can launch its tongue 20 feet in about 20 milliseconds. So if one sticks its tongue out at you, you'll never know it.

January 17

A bacterium found in soil stimulates serotonin production; ergo, if you're feeling low, prune and repot your houseplants. While you're at it, give them a sponge bath or gentle shower to clear their pores. Yes, plants have pores.

January 18

The image entering a cow's eye is about three times brighter than what a human eye sees.

January 19

In an ancient form of divination called **auspicy**, the flight of birds was an important source of information. The sighting of a crow symbolized change, and magpies were believed to be harbingers of good news, as evidenced by this children's rhyme, first transcribed around 1780:

> One for sorrow,
> Two for mirth
> Three for a letter,
> Four for birth,
> Five for silver,
> Six for gold
> And seven for a secret never to be told.

January 20

In 1610, Galileo observed the revolution of Jupiter's four brightest moons, validating the heliocentric concept of the solar system. They're called the Galilean moons in his honor and are breathtaking through a telescope.

January 21

PACKRATS

Bushy-tailed woodrats, commonly called packrats, are compulsively acquisitive. Showing a marked preference for shiny objects, they have been known to glean coins, jewelry, silverware, glasses, dentures and sticks of dynamite. They often leave something behind in place of the pilfered object, not because they are driven to be equitable, but because they get excited and drop their old treasure when they spot a new one.

Packrats feed on leaves, twigs, seeds, fruit, mushrooms and sometimes carrion. When alarmed, they stomp their hind feet in warning. When relaxed, they tap them in a slow, jazzy tempo.

January 22

This is a good time to prune grapevines. Cut them back to the main structure of the plant, leaving two buds per side-shoot.

January 23

In the Middles Ages, **chives** were used as a cure for melancholy. Chive leaves and flowers are high in vitamin C, folic acid and potassium. They contain essential oils that ease stomach distress, stimulate the appetite, aid in fat digestion, protect the heart and boost the immune system.

January 24

Ladies, take note. In an effort to score, **male flies** sometimes dance around prospective mates dangling a silk-wrapped package. If a female accepts the package, the male sneaks in and does the deed while she unwraps it. By the time she's finished, so is he. Rudely enough, the package is sometimes empty.

January 25

It's time to bust out the **seed catalogs** and plan this year's garden. Here's an 83-year-old master gardener's approach to ordering seeds: "First, go crazy. List everything your heart desires; it'll add up to thousands of dollars. Then start crossing things off the list that you really can't afford, don't have space for, or lack the patience to pamper. Pretty soon you'll have a sensible and affordable list."

January 26 It's mating season for raccoons, a few of which probably live in your neighborhood. Studies have found that raccoons understand the abstract principles of locking mechanisms and can figure out how to undo locks (to get into a chicken coop or open a cat door) as quickly as rhesus monkeys.

January 27

In temperate zones, keep your eyes peeled for the first blooming snowdrops and violets.

January 28

Galantamine, a compound found in snowdrops and other narcissi, is used to treat Alzheimer's. It's been suggested that the magical herb *moly,* antidote to Circe's poison in Homer's *Odyssey,* was snowdrop.

January 29

Sweet violet has a long history of use as a cough remedy, especially in the treatment of bronchitis.

January 30

On overcast days, the sun often breaks through the clouds around midday. That's because at noon, the sun is directly overhead rather than at an oblique angle, so the layer of clouds and pollutants it has to penetrate is thinner. It's also 4,000 miles closer to Earth than it is at dawn.

January 31

Southern Tier residents can start planting roses, dogwoods, redbuds, rhododendrons, camellias and azaleas now.

Honey made from some types of rhododendron is slightly hallucinogenic and acts as a laxative, as first discovered by Greek soldiers in 401 B.C. Cases of rhododendron honey madness are still occasionally reported. Rhododendron is extremely toxic to grazing animals, especially horses.

February 1

February takes its name from Februus, the Roman god of purification. To some Native American tribes, this was the month of the Full Snow Moon or Full Hunger Moon.

February 2

Today is Winter Cross-Quarter Day, the midpoint of the winter season in North America, long a day of celebration in northern climes. Canadians and Americans observe it as Groundhog Day, when Punxsutawney Phil is dragged from his burrow to see if he can see his shadow. If he does, expect six more weeks of winter; if he doesn't, spring is nearly here.

For reasons lost in the fog of time, French tradition holds that eating pancakes today prevents hemorrhoids for the rest of the year.

February 3

The ancient Egyptians used the three major stars in Orion's Belt—Alnitak, Alnilam and Mintaka—as a pattern for the alignment and size of the three pyramids at Giza. In the Northern Hemisphere, Orion is visible late fall through winter; in the Southern Hemisphere, late spring through summer.

February 4

Watch for **cedar waxwings** feeding on last year's fruits and berries. A lovely, silky wash of brown, gray, and lemon yellow, cedar waxwings have a low crest, a distinctive black eye mask, and a small, brilliant patch of red on their wings. Highly sociable, they form large flocks that fluidly shrink, grow, divide and rejoin, and often perch in a line and pass berries to one another. To attract waxwings to your yard, plant trees and shrubs that bear small fruits, such as cedar, dogwood, juniper, hawthorn, serviceberry and winterberry.

February 5

Porcupines are found around most urban areas but, being mostly nocturnal, are rarely seen. In summer they dine on berries, roots and stems; in winter on bark and conifer needles. They also gnaw anything salty, including plywood and sweaty shoes, and they frequent roads where rock salt is used. And since they're slow and klutzy, it all too often ends badly. If you have porcupines in your neighborhood, it would be kind to put out a salt lick to keep them away from the road.

February 6

Porcupines aren't clumsy just around vehicles; they regularly fall out of trees while straining to reach a tender bud or twig. Luckily, evolution has compensated for the porcupine's lack of grace: it actually has antibiotics in its skin to prevent infection when it sticks itself with its own quills.

February 7

Venus

Venus may be Earth's sister planet, comparable in size and mass, but she's not really a sister you'd want to visit. Venus's day is longer than its year, and it rotates on its axis almost upside down. Surface temperature is consistently around 850 degrees Fahrenheit, and the suffocatingly dense air contains no oxygen. Venus's clouds are made of white sulfuric acid, which makes the planet highly reflective.

Studies suggest that several billion years ago, Venus's atmosphere was similar to Earth's, and much of its surface was covered by water. But a runaway greenhouse effect generated a critical level of gases in its atmosphere. Hmmm.

February 8

It's avocado season in California, Florida, and Texas. The avocado tree originated in Puebla, Mexico, where it has been cultivated for at least 10,000 years.

Avocado trees are subtropical, tolerating no frost and little wind. Tree leaves and bark are toxic to domestic and wild animals, as are the fruit's skin and pit; so keep everything except the yummy, healthy-fat-filled flesh away from kids and critters.

February 9

Spider Mites thrive in warm, dry indoor conditions. Mist the undersides of houseplants to keep them at bay.

February 10

The avocado is likely an evolutionary anachronism: most large, fleshy fruits co-evolve with an animal big enough to eat it whole and excrete the toxic pit, which subsequently sprouts. As there's no animal in Mexico large enough to slurp down an avocado and poop out the pit, it probably developed in step with one of the Pleisto-cene megafauna, such as *Megatherium,* the giant ground sloth.

February 11

The pigeon, *Columba livia,* was revered by the ancient Greeks, who considered it Aphrodite's totem and a symbol of female sexuality. In India, where it originated, it represents lust.

There is no difference between pigeons and doves except coloration.

February 12

The rice grain-sized **red velvet mite** roams the forest floor, using teeny, tiny lobster-like claws to grab its even more miniscule bacteria- and fungi-eating prey.

As befitting its name and appearance, the red velvet mite is a romantic. When a male decides it's time to meet

that special lady, he creates what entomologists call a "love garden," depositing glistening nodules of sperm atop twigs and stems throughout his territory. He then lays down an intricate silken road leading to his creation and waits for Cupid to strike. If a female happens by and is suitably impressed, she sits on a sperm ball and impregnates herself.

February 14

It's mating season for wolves, foxes, and coyotes.

Lupa, the wolf, was a sacred animal to the Romans, symbolizing the natural breeding cycle. St. Valentine's Day was originally known as Lupercalia, the Roman festival of sexuality.

February 15

The **coyote** is the fastest member of the *canid* family, cruising at a cool 25–30 mph, with bursts of up to 40 mph for short distances. Able to leap 14 feet into the air, it can intercept birds in mid-flight and frogs in mid-hop. Unlike wolves, coyotes always run with their tails down.

February 16

Snow fleas, also called springtails, rise to the surface of the snow around bases of trees as temperatures warm. They're not really fleas; they just hop around like them as they dine on algae, bacteria and fungi.

February 17

This is a great time to pull perennial weeds, like plantain, crabgrass, and **mallow.**

Common mallow, also called cheeseweed, is a member of the genus *Malva,* for which the color mauve was named. Though generally considered a weed, it's both edible and medicinal. Young leaves can be eaten as a green—cooked or raw—or as a thickener for soup. Early Native Americans used mallow to heal skin irritations; they also processed dye from it and used the roots as toothbrushes.

February 18

If the temperature is above freezing in your area, you can prune fruit trees now, as well as honeysuckle, clematis, holly, and grapevines.

February 19

The last insect to go in winter and first to show in spring, the housefly is a good harbinger of coming seasons. Yes, houseflies are gross, but they're cool, too. Their antennae sport feather-like projections that act as wind speed indicators, and their feet have hairy little pads called *pulvilli* that secrete a gooey liquid that enables them to cling to virtually anything.

Houseflies also have a built-in straw, used to suck up food that they've just liquefied by spitting on it through the same tube. Try not to think about that next time one lands on your sandwich.

February 20

There are upwards of 170 billion galaxies in the known universe. The galaxies nearest our Milky Way are the Canis Major and Sagittarius dwarf galaxies. Andromeda, the nearest spiral galaxy, is the brightest galaxy visible from the Northern Hemisphere and can often be seen through a small telescope.

February 21

Milbert's tortoiseshell and brown mourning cloak butterflies are emerging from hibernation and feeding on tree sap and bird droppings. Both species resemble dead leaves when their wings are folded, but their open wings have bright bands and spots that shimmer and glow in the early spring sun.

February 22

The Northeast is in the midst of the **maple-sugaring season**. Sugar maple leaves, which turn glorious shades of red and orange in the fall, have five distinct lobes and a smooth underside. Sugar is produced in those lovely leaves via photosynthesis. It is then transported into the wood, where it converts into sucrose and dissolves into the sap. In early spring, when frigid nights are followed by sunny, above-freezing days, the sap begins to flow. The flow stops whenever nighttime temperatures rise above freezing or daytime temperatures fail to.

Besides sugar maples, silver and red maples can be tapped, as well as box elder, walnut, hickory, sycamore and sweet birch trees.

Double samara (winged seed)

Sugar maple bud

February 23

In temperate zones, now is the time to start seeds for cool-weather veggies such as broccoli, Brussels sprouts, cabbage, cauliflower, leeks, lettuce, mizuna, onions and spinach. Plant near a sunny window, under grow lights, or in a greenhouse or cloche.

February 24

Cabbage is an example of a polymorphic plant, one that can take different forms. The original wild cabbage plant, native to coastal southern and western Europe, has morphed into heading cabbage, non-heading kale, kohlrabi, Brussels sprouts, broccoli and cauliflower. If grown in proximity, all six will cross-pollinate and after several seasons, revert to their wild-cabbage roots. In the garden, keep them as far apart as possible.

February 25

If you live in the Southern Tier, you can now start planting beets, broccoli, cabbage, carrots, cauliflower, chard, endive, kale, onions, peas, potatoes, radishes, spinach and turnips.

February 26

CROCUS

In temperate areas, keep an eye out for blooming snowdrops, violets and crocus.

Saffron, the world's most expensive spice, is derived from the flower of the saffron crocus, a sterile, autumn-flowering perennial that thrives in arid lands. Saffron has been used in cooking, medicine and art for over 50,000 years. It has long been touted as a remedy for depression; so if the winter blues are getting you down, try a lovely, tasty bowl of saffron-infused rice.

February 27

Some **violets** contain a compound that temporarily desensitizes scent receptors in the nose, preventing you from smelling it again until your nerves recover. Perfumers often use the compound to prevent scents from being too overpowering.

February 28

Mourning doves, house finches, meadowlarks and red-winged blackbirds are beginning to sing. Bluebirds are returning to their summer ranges.

If you'd like to attract bluebirds, put out a nesting box along with a platform feeder filled with mealworms or raisins soaked in water. Birds also appreciate heated birdbaths.

February 29

Jumping Spiders

Male jumping spiders have to provide lots of visual signals to avoid becoming lunch. Unlike the rather drab—and apparently snappish—female, the male sports swollen, psychedelic pedipalps, a funky goatee and crazy-long multicolored front legs. He approaches the female doing an arachnid version of the jerk, with front legs raised and pedipalps waving, hoping to either impress, amuse, or distract her from eating him.

It's been found that jumping spiders, which have excellent vision and often dwell inside homes, watch television and react to on-screen images of other spiders and flies. If you live in the West, it's wise to cultivate a family of jumping spiders in your home, as they are the only predator of the highly poisonous hobo spider. Plus, they're cool to look at and fun to watch as they bungee jump on silken threads and stalk their prey.

JANUARY
FEBRUARY
MARCH
APRIL
MAY
JUNE
JULY
AUGUST
SEPTEMBER
OCTOBER
NOVEMBER
DECEMBER

March 1

March takes its name from Mars, the Roman god of crops, vegetation and war. In times past, this was the New Year, celebrated in conjunction with the beginning of spring. To Native Americans, this was the month of the Full Worm Moon, because worm castings begin to appear, signaling that worms and other creatures are moving toward the surface as the soils warms.

March 2

The constellation **Leo, the lion**, is rising in the east at the beginning of the month, so March "comes in like a lion." Aries, the ram, sets in the west at the end of the month, "going out like a lamb."

March 3

In the Southern Tier, it's time to start nightshade seedlings—eggplant, pepper, and tomato. Water newly started seeds and seedlings carefully and with warm water.

March 4

While the trees are still bare, take a walk and look for bird nests. The most common types are:

- Cup nests—most songbirds
- Pendulous/pensile nests—orioles, vireos
- Cavity nests—woodpeckers, some nuthatches
- Platform nests—osprey, eagles, and some hawks

Many birds weave aromatic plants into their nests to keep them clean and bug-free.

March 5

Step outside and face north tonight. Going roughly clockwise from the zenith, here are some of the constellations you'll see: Ursa Major, Ursa Minor, Draco, Cepheus, Lacerta, Andromeda, Cassiopeia and Aurgia.

Face south and see: Gemini, Canis Minor, Orion, Lepus, Canis Major, and Leo.

March 6
Snowshoe Hares

The old saying "mad as a March hare" originally referred to the brown hares of England, which get frisky during mating this month. But their behavior is nothing compared to the freaky show put on by the snowshoe hare. Mating male snowshoes chase, kick, bite, hiss and urinate on other males, and they perform a bizarre— and surprisingly noisy—courtship ritual that includes a great deal of forward and backward jumping, more urinating, midair spinning and snake-like hissing. Snowshoes are a popular treat for foxes, coyotes, bobcats, bears and raptors, and are thus known among wildlife biologists as the "Snickers bars of the forest."

March 7

In all zones, this is a good month to plant trees and shrubs.

Yew pines, mulberry, birch, bottlebrush and **junipers** produce prodigious amounts of pollen, so if you have allergies, you might choose other varieties. And burning bushes really do burn: they produce enough volatile oil that lighting a match nearby can set them on fire.

If you're thinking about planting a fruit tree, keep in mind that apple, pear, cherry and most plum trees need to cross-pollinate with another tree. Apricots (some varieties), peaches, plums and nectarines can self-pollinate.

March 8

The earth, like the sea, rises and falls several inches over the course of a day, thanks to the same gravitational forces that cause ocean tides.

March 9

This is the month to feed lawns with slow-release organic fertilizer or mulch. While you're at it, pay attention to what the weeds are telling you:

- Crabgrass suggests you mow too low or too often
- Clover indicates insufficient nitrogen
- Dandelions prefer high-acid soil
- Quackgrass likes thin, poorly watered soil
- Ground ivy thrives when there's too little sun
- Knotweed says your soil is compressed
- Buttercups love overly wet hardpan

March 10

Insects are programmed to appear just when their favorite plants are available, so planting just a little off cycle can protect vegetables from common pests. Plant carrots and corn later in the spring to avoid carrot maggots and corn borers, and plant cabbage and potatoes early to dodge cabbage loopers and leafhoppers.

March 11

Mourning doves are singing, nesting and mating. The male mourning dove gathers nesting materials and then stands on the female's back to deliver them, piece by piece, waiting patiently as she weaves each one in. It's fortunate that mourning doves are wildly prolific—a pair can raise up to six broods per year—as they're the most heavily hunted game bird the U.S. They're also monogamous, affectionate and very good parents, with both the male and female producing crop milk for the nestlings.

March 12

Dandelion greens are tender and tasty now. The English folk name for dandelion is piss-a-bed, for the strong diuretic effect of its roots. In French, it's *pisse au lit*.

March 13

The **American kestrel**, also known as the sparrow hawk, is the most common falcon in North America. Small, feisty and fierce, it's well adapted to urban life. It can often be spotted atop utility poles, pumping its rust-colored tail up and down and uttering a shrill *"killy-killy-killy-killy."* The kestrel hunts in fields and open areas, hovering 33 to 66 feet above the ground. Spotting a tasty rodent, lizard or large insect, it does an abrupt, kamikaze-type stoop. Like all falcons, kestrels have a tomial, or falcon, tooth that is used to sever the spinal column of its prey.

If you live on the edge of even a small open area, you should build or buy a kestrel nesting box. Kestrels are attentive and hard-working parents, and watching a clutch of babies fledge and learn to hunt is an amazing experience. Kestrel families tend to return to the same nest box year after year.

March 14

Garden work can begin when a lump of soil squeezed in the hand is dry enough to fall apart slowly. If the soil is wet and slow to dry, you can cover beds with black plastic mulch for a week or so to speed things up.

March 15

Bees are starting to venture out of the hive in search of food.

March 16

It's time to plant early crops when the lilacs show their first leaves or when the **daffodils** start to bloom.

Early crops include carrots, celery, collards, leeks, lettuce, mixed greens, onions, parsley, parsnips, potatoes, radishes, snow peas, Swiss chard and turnips, along with larkspur, pansies, poppies, sweet peas, wildflowers, evergreen trees and shrubs. Radishes and peas are the most cold-hardy of vegetables; if the weather is still wintry, start with just those.

To improve germination, soak pea seeds overnight in lukewarm water before planting.

March 17

You'd think that the
bed bug would
be good in bed,
but any creature
that reproduces
using a method
called **traumatic
insemination**
is guaranteed to be
lacking in finesse. But,
then, the female bed bug has
no genital opening, a situation that does oblige
brute force. Foreplay, therefore, consists of the
male punching a hole through the female's body
wall. Once inside, he pumps sperm directly into her
bloodstream; the sperm then wanders haphazardly
through her system until it bumps into her reproduc-
tive organs. Unsurprisingly, this indelicate process
leaves the female with a nasty scar, thus marking her
as an experienced bug.

Although they are scarcer than they once were,
the flat and beaky bed bugs can still be found where
many mammals slumber, either *en mass* or serially.
The bugs don't actually dwell in beds, but in nearby

nooks and crannies, from which they venture forth after dark, using a thermoreceptor to locate prey.

The bed bug's natural foe is the masked bedbug hunter, an insect resembling a predatory dust ball.

The word *bug* was coined expressly for the bed bug sometime in the itchy Middle Ages. Also, the French adjective *punaise,* meaning "stinking," was conceived specifically to describe the noxious body odor exuded by the bed bug, a cachet surely no other bug can claim.

March 18
In Norse legend, peas were sent to earth by the god Thor, who ordered his dragons to drop them in the wells of unworthy humans. Some of the peas accidentally fell to the ground and sprouted. Norsemen therefore only ate peas on Thor's day—Thursday.

March 19

In Amazonian culture, it's traditional to close your mouth when you see a rainbow, because rainbows harbor malign spirits that sneak in that way.

March 20
Vernal Equinox

The sun crosses the celestial equator from south to north today. On both the Vernal and Autumnal Equinoxes, the sun rises exactly in the east, travels across the sky for 12 hours, and sets exactly in the west, giving every place on Earth an equally balanced night and day.

March 21
First Day of Spring

Spring moves north at about 16 miles per day, or 100 miles per week. It moves uphill only about 100 feet per day, thus arriving later at higher altitudes.

March 22

In the non-temperate zones, crocus, daffodils, snowdrops and forsythia are blooming.

March 23

Forsythia originated in China and was first sent to Europe in 1842 by

a British collector of exotic plants named Robert Fortune. In his nineteen years traveling the Orient to collect specimens, the unfortunate Fortune was waylaid by pirates, shipwrecked, felled by sunstroke, and repeatedly robbed and beaten.

March 24

Fertile, well-balanced soil contains up to 2 million **earthworms** per acre—a fact not surprising when one takes into account that each worm is hermaphroditic, able to mate twice at the same time. This makes for strange genealogy, as one worm's mother could be its siblings' father.

March 25

Compared with other moons in our solar system, Earth's moon is something of an oddity. All the other planets are much larger than their moons, especially Jupiter and Saturn, which are 40 or 50 times larger than their biggest satellites. Earth, at only about four times wider, could almost be considered a twin to its moon.

March 26

If a jet flying overhead

doesn't leave a visible contrail, it
probably won't rain the next day.

March 27

Time to plant kale!

In non-temperate
zones, it's time to plant
beets, broccoli, Brussels sprouts, cabbage,
cauliflower, kale, and
spinach.

March 28

It is said that the Greeks offered **beet greens** to Apollo on a silver platter at the temple of Delphi. Old Russian healers believed that beets could cure tuberculosis, scurvy and toothache and could even double as an insecticide. Conversely, an old Ukrainian proverb warns, "A tale that begins with a beet will end with the devil."

March 29

It's time to repot and begin fertilizing houseplants again. A stinky mix of liquid fish emulsion and apple cider vinegar does wonders.

March 30

To maximize garden space, sow long- and short-season vegetables close together; the short-term crop will be harvested by time the long-term one needs room. Good combos include:

- **Radishes and cabbage**
- **Chinese cabbage and eggplant**
- **Lettuce and turnips**
- **Radishes and beans.**

The early Egyptians, Greeks, and Romans used the bitter sap exuded by lettuce as a mild narcotic, similar to laudanum.

March 31

Female songbirds prefer males with large repertoires and choose to mate with the male that can sing the widest range of tunes. It's thought that the ability to memorize songs is linked to the size of the spleen, which, in turn, is connected to the quality of the immune system.

April 1

April, or *Aprilis*, was the Roman name for Aphrodite, the goddess of love and transformation, and it is rooted in the Latin verb *aperies*, "to open." To early Native American coastal tribes, it was the month of the Full Fish Moon, as this was the month that the shad swam upstream to spawn.

April 2

TREES

Trees are humankind's best friends. They remove carbon dioxide (CO_2) from the atmosphere via photosynthesis, store it as cellulose in their trunks, branches, leaves and roots, and release oxygen back into the air as a byproduct. They also cool our cities and homes and reduce energy usage. Pines and other evergreens planted on the north side of a home serve as a wind block during cold months. Deciduous trees planted on the south side provide shade in the summer but don't block out light in the winter.

April 3

Facing the north sky tonight and going roughly clockwise from the zenith, here are some of the constellations you can see: Ursa Major, Botes, Draco, Lacerta, Cepheus, Cassiopeia, Perseus and Auriga. Face south and see Leo Minor, Gemini, Cancer, Canis Minor, Canis Major, Corvus, Virgo and Leo.

April 4

It's time to clear winter mulch from around roses and give them a good cutting and feeding. Roses love old bananas and egg shells worked into the soil.

This is also a good time to plant raspberries and blackberries. Berries thrive on acid, so mulch them with pine needles.

April 5

Healthy garden soil has the same characteristics as a good chocolate cake: it is dark and rich in color, springy yet crumby, and smells wonderful! The magic ingredient in healthy soil is **humus**, a slimy brown substance made up of decomposed plants, critters and bacteria. Compost is the best source of humus.

April 6

Baby raccoons, porcupines, and red foxes are being born.

April 7

The daytime high temperature on the **_moon_** can reach 243 degrees Fahrenheit, while the nighttime can plummet to minus 272. Temperatures are extreme because there isn't enough atmosphere to insulate the surface.

April 8

A PROPER BIRD BOX

If you put out a bird nest box and nobody moves in the first year, don't give up; you'll probably get takers the second nesting season. Make sure the nest box is made of untreated wood, doesn't have a perch (so other birds aren't tempted to land there), is protected from wind, rain and full sun (chicks die if they get overheated), and doesn't contain any nesting materials (birds like to provide their own).

April 9

Birds pass on songs from generation to generation, often on a gender basis—males to sons, females to daughters.

April 10

Are apple blossoms budding? If they are, it's time to plant arugula, asparagus, beets, broccoli, Brussels sprouts, cabbage, cauliflower, cilantro, dill, kohlrabi and spinach. You can also still plant carrots, celery, collards, leeks, lettuce, mixed greens, onions, parsley, parsnips, potatoes, radishes, snow peas, Swiss chard and turnips if you haven't yet.

When planting, consider that carrots and tomatoes don't grow well near each other. Neither do squash and potatoes, lettuce and broccoli, or peppers and beans.

April 11

COMPOST MADE E-Z:

To create a compost pile, simply start mixing together **green waste** (grass clippings, weeds, manure, vegetable scraps, and coffee grounds) and **brown waste** (dry leaves, straw, wood shavings, paper, dried corn, and sunflower stems). The amount of green to brown should be almost even, with just slightly more green. If the carbon (brown) to nitrogen (green), or C/N, ratio is too high, decomposition will be slow; if it's too low, nitrogen will escape, and the pile will smell bad.

Keep the pile moist but not soggy, and turn it monthly—if you can. If turning it is too difficult physically, don't worry: you'll still get compost; it will just take longer.

April 12

Some wild plants, like stinging nettle, appear in early spring so they can soak up lots of sun before the trees leaf out and shade them.

April 13

The Roman festival of Ceres, goddess of the crops, was once celebrated on this date. Farmers would whirl and leap through the fields with lighted torches, a move that morphed into the "stag leap" in ballet.

April 14

When deciding on flowers for your garden, consider which colors your favorite pollinators prefer:

- **Bees** see yellow, blue, purple, and ultraviolet.
- **Butterflies** look for red, orange, yellow, and pink.
- **Hummingbirds** hone in on red, orange, and purple.

April 15

Astrological gardeners believe the moon controls the moisture in soil, just as it does the tides. Moisture content is said to be at its peak during the new moon and full moon, when tides are highest, making those the best times to plant.

April 16

Golden eagle chicks are hatching. It takes about 100 days for an eagle hatchling to become independent. Mortality in juvenile eagles is as high as 75 percent, so it can take one mating pair up to nineteen years to produce just two breeding offspring.

April 17

The spirals on **snail shells** form proportionally in the golden ratio, which means each new compartment is larger than the one before it by an exact and constant factor. Most snails have whorls only on their right side; left-sided snails are extremely rare.

April 18

Bird parents load their chicks up with spiders during the mid-point of their development. Spiders are loaded with taurine, an amino acid needed to develop visual acuity, intelligence and resistance to anxiety.

Cats need taurine, too, or they'll go blind, which is a good reason not to feed your cat dog food.

April 19

Raindrops constantly change shape as they fall.

The sources of the heavenly scent during and immediately after it rains are petrichor and geosmin. **Petricor** is an oil produced by plants then absorbed by rocks and soil and released into the air during rainfall. The word *petricor* comes from *petros,* Greek for stone, and *ichor,* the earthy yet divine fluid flowing through the veins of the gods.

Geosmin, which translates to "earth smell," is an organic compound produced by soil microbes. It gives beets, carp and catfish their dense, earthy flavors, and when mixed with petricor produces a fleeting but exquisite aroma. It seems that the scent of geosmin is pleasure that's wired into the human brain; we can detect it at concentrations as low as five parts per billion.

April 20

The **potato** began as a nut-sized, starchy tuber growing wild in the sparse soil and rarefied air of the Andean *altiplano*. The early Inca were no doubt delighted to discover a native food plant that thrived at high altitudes, in extreme weather, on nearly vertical slopes. They eventually developed 3,000 distinct varieties in a rainbow of colors, textures, tastes, sizes and shapes, all suited to different conditions.

Potatoes need plenty of light and moisture and prefer slightly acid soil. To plant, dig a trench 5 inches deep and 30–36 inches wide, and place a tuber every 12–14 inches. Cover with soil, and follow with a mulch of straw or hay at least 10 inches deep. Add more mulch as the vines grow through the first layer, to keep the tubers covered. (Tubers develop a mildly toxic substance called solanine when exposed to sunlight.) Once the plants blossom, stop covering them completely, but mulch well all around.

You can also grow potatoes in bushel baskets or five-gallon pails with holes punched in the bottom. Fill the container halfway with compost, set the potatoes, and cover. Keep adding compost as they grow, making sure to keep them covered.

April 21

Anthocyanin, found in black turtle beans, purple cabbage, eggplant, potatoes, red onions, red and purple grapes and berries, may help prevent or reverse both age-related cognitive decline and insulin resistance.

April 22

When planting, don't add amendments to the hole; use the native soil, then add amendments as topdressing. Amendments in the hole will inhibit root growth and disrupt water movement. Don't add manure, in particular, as it will burn the roots.

Butterflies

require warmth to fly, so most butterflies active in the early spring—such as mourning cloaks, melissa blues, painted ladies, and red admirals—have dark wings that absorb solar heat.

Want to create a butterfly-friendly yard? Here are the essential elements:

- **Butterflies need a windbreak** near their feeding place, so they won't be blown about as they eat. Any hedge or wall will do.

- **They need food,** usually in the form of nectar. Asters, bee balm, butterfly bush, butterfly plant, potentilla, chokecherry, cosmos, dill, fennel, hollyhock, marigold, milkweed, mustard, parsley, rabbit brush, sunflower, sweet pea, thistle, verbena, and zinnia are all good nectar-bearers, and they require little water and are low maintenance. But not all butterflies are nectar-feeders; members of the *Nymphalidae* family feed on sap, rotting fruit and animal dung.

- **Butterflies also need water,** which they prefer in the form of a damp spot or puddle from which they can absorb minerals as well as water. You can create a butterfly puddle by piling sand in a pie plate or other shallow pan, and filling it three-quarters full of water. If you really want to reel 'em in, toss in a piece of horse poop.

Just remember, butterflies are caterpillars first, and caterpillars feed on vegetables, flowers, and herbs. But so what if your plants get munched a bit? It'll be worth it to see your garden gorgeously a-flutter.

April 24

In non-temperate climes, it's time to start prepping beds for warm-weather crops; healthy soil needs 2 to 3 inches of new compost, depleted soil 4 to 6 inches. You could also add dry or liquid molasses to stimulate the soil microbes. Molasses works well as a foliar spray, too, and will kick-start your compost pile.

April 25

When the barometric pressure drops, swallows fly as close to the ground as possible, where air density is greatest. Low-flying birds are a sign of imminent rain; high flyers, fair weather.

April 26

A "sagan" is a unit of measurement used by astronomers to mean **"at least 4 billion."**

April 27 Talk about fabulous choreography: During the winter, the buds of trees are prevented from growing by a chemical inhibitor that gradually breaks down as the season progresses. Once the inhibitor breaks down, the buds develop at a rate determined by the accumulating warmth of spring. As the leaves unfurl, the insects that feed on the leaves start to hatch, and the birds that feed on those insects return from migration. A good example is the spring cankerworm, which feeds on box elder leaves and is, in turn, fed upon by the gorgeous orioles that make their summer homes in temperate climates.

April 28

Seeds contain their own food supply and rot if planted in too-rich soil. Wait until seedlings have sprouted their first leaves to enrich the soil with compost or fertilizer.

April 29

When handling a seedling, pick it up by the leaves, not the stem, and support the little root ball with your hand. If you break the fragile stem, the plant will die, but if you break a couple of leaves, they'll grow back.

April 30
Plants exude scented oils that enter into the soil, and when the relative humidity of the soil reaches 75 percent or greater, the scent of those oils is released into the air. **That's why the world smells so good in spring.**

May 1

Today is **Spring Cross-Quarter Day,** the midpoint between spring and summer. May takes its name from Maia, the Goddess of Spring, also known as Artemis or Diana, She Who Brings Forth Life. To some early Native American tribes, this was the month of the Full Flower, for the abundance of blooming plants, or Full Corn Planting Moon.

May 2

In the north sky tonight, roughly clockwise from the zenith, you can see Hercules, Draco, Lyra, Cygnus, Cassiopeia, Perseus, Auriga, Ursa Major and Leo Minor. Facing south, look for Corvus, Lupus, Scorpius, Virgo, Ophiuchus and Boötes.

May 3

Mayflies are, by necessity, the ultimate proponents of *carpe diem*. The adult mayfly, whose order name *Ephemeroptera* means "living a day," bursts from the water at dawn and by nightfall returns—dead. It's an action-packed day, to say

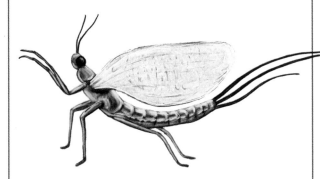

the least, filled with hatching, dancing, copulating, giving birth and dying. Perhaps that's why male mayflies have two penises and females have two vaginas—so they can do it double time. Mayflies are important bio-indicators, as their naiads are unable to survive in streams polluted by heavy metals or pesticides.

May 4

In coastal California, this is the season of the "May gray," soon to be followed by "June gloom," when the **marine layer**—an air mass that develops over the ocean and is propelled inland by rising heat—tends to toss a blanket of cool, sometimes foggy, air over normally sunny regions. The marine layer itself isn't fog, but clouds and fog can develop within it under the right circumstances.

May 5

Not sure where to put your vegetable garden? The answer is in the weeds: Dandelion, cornflower, puncture vine, and small nettle thrive in the kind of well-drained, sandy soil best suited for vegetable gardens.

May 6

The Eta Aquarid
meteor shower
peaks tonight.
Meteor showers
occur when the
debris stream from
a comet enters Earth's
atmosphere. Both the Eta Aquarids
and November's Orionids are born
of Halley's Comet, which will next be
visible in mid-2061.

May 7 Each spring, hundreds of thousands
of **American shad**, a sleek,
silvery herring, leave the open ocean and swarm into
New York Harbor on their way to their Hudson River
spawning grounds. Shad can reach lengths of $2^1/_2$
feet, and weigh up to nine pounds.

May 8

DON'T HAVE TIME OR SPACE FOR A

VEGETABLE GARDEN

but want a steady supply of fresh, locally grown produce? Buy a share from one of your local **Community Supported Agriculture** (CSA) farms.

CSA is a model of mutually supportive local agriculture. Each year, before the crops are sown, members of the CSA pay the farmer for "shares" of the coming seasons' harvest. It's a beneficial arrangement for both buyers and growers: the former is guaranteed a bounty of fresh, organic produce, and the latter, an infusion of income early in the season, when it's needed the most.

May 9

Birds have a reflex that makes them pause between swallowings, so if a worm is put in the mouth of a just-fed chick, it will sit there for a while and the parent will know to pull it back out and give it to a different chick.

Baby birds create their own diapers—fecal sacs containing their waste—which the parents drop outside the nest.

May 10

In temperate climes, a period of unseasonable cold called "blackberry winter" often falls around now, when blackberries are in bloom.

When planning your garden, keep in mind that cold air flows downhill, so heat-loving crops, like tomatoes, eggplant, and peppers, should be planted at the highest point in the yard.

May 11

FROGS!

Frogs and toads are singing and mating. The love song of the leopard frog has been likened to the sound of a wet hand being rubbed over a tightly inflated balloon. Not exactly Barry White, but then male leopard frogs aren't known as the Lotharios of the amphibian world. Eternally hopeful and utterly clueless, they attempt to mate with anything that moves, including indignant turtles and floating leaves. When an actual female frog is located, the male must dig his specially adapted thumbs into her back to keep her from wandering off in boredom. Trapped in his clumsy, clammy embrace, the female lays a loose oval mass of approximately 3,000 eggs, which the male fertilizes. Both then hop off and leave the eggs, which in two or three weeks hatch into tadpoles.

May 12
In temperate zones, it's time to plant eggplant, pumpkins, summer squash, winter squash, tomatoes, and watermelon, as well as cosmos, gladiolas, marigolds, mums, Shasta daisies, sunflowers, zinnias, and other heat-loving flowers.

May 13

Don't plant **sunflowers** too near other flowers or vegetables. The roots of sunflowers (like those of the black walnut tree) release toxins that inhibit the growth of nearby plants. This phenomenon, called allelopathy, is a great method of organic weed control, but it can wreak havoc if you allow sunflowers to grow randomly throughout your yard.

May 14

Alligator raves? On warm spring nights, large numbers of American alligators gather for group courtship in so-called "alligator dances." And while that may sound like a recipe for reptilian promiscuity, it's been discovered that female alligators, at least, are serially monogamous, returning to the same mate for many years.

And unlike most reptiles, American alligators are good mothers, keeping their eggs warm, helping the young hatch, and protecting them for their first five months.

May 15

Despite the fact that they have no vocal cords, male alligators manage to make plenty of noise during courtship, sucking air into their lungs and blowing it out in intermittent, deep-toned bellows. They also use infrasound (sound lower in frequency than humans can typically hear), the low rumbling causing the water directly over their backs to oscillate in a lovely liquid dance.

May 16

Planting a bed of blue flowers at the perimeter will make your yard look larger.

May 17

Atmosphere pressure is so low on Mars that temperatures decrease by as much as 18 degrees from the surface to a height of just three feet.

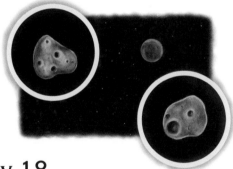

May 18

Mars has two small, weirdly shaped moons, **Phobos** (fear) and **Deimos** (panic), named for the horses that pulled the chariot of Ares, the Greek god of war (counterpart to the Roman Mars).

May 19

Noting that petals open and close at the same time each day, the eighteenth-century botanist Carl Linnaeus arranged flowers in sequence, using the movement of their petals as a floral clock.

May 20

Many insects have **aposematic coloration**, which advertises that they taste bad or have defensive abilities—though some are just faking. Orange and black is one of the more popular aposematic color schemes, shared by Monarch butterflies and ladybugs, both of which taste nasty, as well as various stinging wasps. Syrphid flies, too, are orange and black but neither taste bad nor have defensive bites or stings.

May 21

Artemisia absinthium is a species of wormwood native to Africa and Eurasia, but now naturalized through much of North America. It's the primary ingredient in absinthe, an alcoholic spirit historically referred to as *la fée verte,* or the Green Fairy. (Van Gogh is said to have been drinking absinthe when he cut off his ear.) Planted around garden borders, lovely, feathery Artemisia will repel both pests and weeds. Inside, its dried leaves protect against moths.

May 22

The crescent moon is always low in the sky and visible only near dawn or dusk. When it appears, the dark portion seems to glow, a phenomenon called **earthshine**. Earthshine occurs because 38 percent of the sunlight that strikes Earth bounces back into space, and some of it bounces again off the lunar surface.

May 23

Young birds need lots of energy when they're first learning to fly, and would benefit from a snack of milk-and-sugar soaked bread, mashed bananas, or cottage cheese with raisins.

May 24

Reflective surfaces disorient aphids, moths and thrips, preventing them from landing. A gazing ball or other piece of reflective garden art near your rose bushes will do more than just look pretty.

May 25

The ten-lined **June beetle**, a type of scarab beetle, is emerging from underground. June beetles spend up to three years as larvae, burrowing down deep into the soil in winter and rising nearer the surface each spring  to feed on grass, potato, and strawberry roots. The almond-sized adult is greenish brown-and-white striped and hisses when disturbed. Though it can deliver an impressive bite, the June beetle is an herbivore, dining exclusively on conifer needles. Like many nocturnal insects, June beetles use the moon and bright stars to navigate but often become confused by unnatural light sources and end up bumping around porch lights or attached to screen doors.

May 26

Peonies secrete a sweet, nutritious nectar designed to lure ants to their buds. The ants protect the about-to-blossom flowers and dine while they do it. As soon as the flowers open, the ants leave.

May 27

Bindweed, a member of the morning glory family, is one of the gardener's worst enemies, with its 18-foot-deep taproots, 10-foot-long side shoots, and seeds that remain viable for half a century. To keep this hydra-headed creeper under control, dig up as much of the root system as you can, spray the leaves (repeatedly) with vinegar or clove oil, and smother it with heavy plantings of taller plants (alfalfa works quite well) throughout the growing season. You can also plant pumpkins; they're the only veggie that can compete.

May 28

Ladybugs

Ladybugs bought in nurseries or online are harvested in the high mountains of the West and Northwest, where they go to feed on pollen. After gorging for a week or two, they mass together in protected places near streams to wait out the summer drought.

May 29 Plants often respond to microbial or viral attacks by killing their own cells—causing localized yellow, brown or mottled spots—around the point of infection, to prevent the disease from spreading to other areas.

May 30

There are about 1,200 species of hawk moths (also called sphinx moths), some of which are easily mistaken for hummingbirds, as they hover in midair to feed on nectar. Many orchids can only be fertilized by hawk moths, which have proboscises as long as or longer than their bodies to reach the nectaries of long-necked flowers.

Hawk moth caterpillars are notorious plant munchers—most notably the comely, plump, green tomato hornworm, larvae of the five-spotted hawk moth—but, hey, everybody has to eat!

May 31

Strawberries mulched with pine needles taste better. Strawberries belong to the rose family, and do resemble rose hips when you look at them in that light. The strawberry as we know it was first hybridized in eighteenth-century France, from wild species found in Virginia and South America.

June 1

June is named for Juno, the Summer Queen, a goddess pregnant with hope, opportunity and the coming harvest. To early Native Americans, this was the month of the Full Rose Moon or Full Hot Moon.

June 2

FIREFLIES (also called glowworms and lightning bugs) generally emit light to attract mates, though some also glow to defend territory and warn predators of their fatal charms (most contain toxins similar to those found in poisonous toads). In most firefly species, both sexes glow, though often only the male flies and flashes, while the female sits back and waits for that special guy to light her up. Scientists have yet to figure out why some fireflies synchronize their flashes among large groups. Annual flash fests occur this time of year in Tennessee's Great Smoky Mountains and Congaree National Park in South Carolina. Fireflies are found in warm, humid areas east of the Rocky Mountains.

To attract fireflies to your yard:

- Never use pesticides.
- Avoid using outside lights.
- Let the leaf litter from trees accumulate.
- Create a water feature.
- Use only organic fertilizer.
- Adjust your lawn mower to the highest setting; ideally three inches.
- Add lots of compost to your soil. This will create a thriving earthworm population for the larvae to feed on.

June 3

Short on gardening space? You can grow snap beans, broccoli, carrots, cucumbers, eggplant, herbs, lettuce, onions, peppers, potatoes, radishes, and tomatoes in window boxes, pots or buckets.

Provide at least five hours of full sun, fertilize twice a month with fish emulsion, and water well and often. And make sure there's room for good air circulation between containers.

While clay pots look nice, they lose water too quickly; you can get around that by slipping a plain plastic pot inside a pretty clay one. Punch a hole in the bottom of the plastic pot for drainage.

June 4

Constellations in the north sky tonight, roughly clockwise from the zenith, are Botes, Hercules, Lyra, Cygnus, Cepheus, Cassiopeia, Perseus, Ursa Minor, Auriga, and Ursa Major.

In the south you'll see Virgo, Centaurus, Lupus, Libra, Scorpius, Sagittarius, Serpens and Corona Borealis.

June 5 When the plant label says "full sun," that means it requires a minimum of six hours of direct sunlight.

June 6

Tired of mowing the lawn? Dig it up and plant thyme. Thyme needs less water than grass, and it smells better too. Mixing different varieties will give your thyme lawn the texture and color of a tapestry. Use varieties of similar height, and plant them in groupings of five or more. 'Albus', 'Coccineus', 'Pink Chintz' and 'Reiter' are often used in mass plantings. Initially, it will need a good soaking once or twice a week; once it's established, you can cut back to every ten days or so.

June 7

The **green darner dragonfly** is common to the United States and southern Canada. Its Latin name, *Anax junius,* translates to Lord of June.

June 8

The Cassini spacecraft continues to discover strange and wondrous things about Saturn and its many moons—over 60 so far. On jumbo-sized Titan, in an Earth-like cycle that uses methane instead of water, spring showers bring methane rains to equatorial deserts. Enceladus, which would comfortably fit between Los Angeles and San Francisco, has huge, ice-shooting geysers. And on freaky, potato-looking Hyperion, days are never the same length and the North Pole rarely points north.

June 9

Planting **perennial herbs** near the house makes it convenient to use them. Mediterranean herbs, including rosemary, oregano, and thyme, are tough—they don't need good soil or much water.

June 10

Different types of **waterfowl** can live and feed in the same area, because variations in neck length and bill shape allow them to feed on divergent food sources. Canada geese, for example, have long necks and broad bills, so they can shear off the tops of small plants growing along the shoreline, while ducks, with their shorter necks, feed on water plants.

June 11

Start looking for the moon during the day. The only time it's not visible is around the new moon.

June 12
Leeches!

A typical backyard pond contains ten different species of leeches, most of which eat midges, worms and each other.

However, should a leech happen to grab hold of you, pry it off with a flat, blunt object. Using heat or chemicals will cause the leech to vomit into the wound before it drops off. And you probably don't want leech barf in your system.

June 13

Some long-rooted plants act like artesian wells, drawing nutrients from the subsoil up to where shallow-rooted plants can access them. Comfrey accumulates potash, nitrogen, calcium and magnesium, and so makes a great neighbor for needy vegetables.

June 14

The word *caterpillar* is based on the Latin *catta pilosa,* which means hairy cat. As a general rule, fuzzy caterpillars turn into moths, and hairless ones become butterflies.

Caterpillars are such big-time poopers that there's a special name for it: **frass**. Unlike eastern tent caterpillars, which frass all over their nests, the caterpillar of the silver-spotted skipper blasts its frass five feet outside its nest. This impressive fecal feat prevents a frass-trail-following predatory wasp from zeroing in on its location.

June 15 When the barometric pressure drops, birds fly as close to the ground as possible, where air density is greatest. So low-flying birds are a sign of imminent rain.

Other **signs of imminent rain**: scurrying ants, biting gnats, unusually loud crickets, spiders coming down from their webs, and flies gathering inside.

June 16
You can lure insects away from outdoor gatherings by coating a few small pieces of cardboard (or anything else) with syrup, and placing them around the perimeter of your patio or yard. The wasps, bees and yellow jackets will have their own party and leave yours alone.

June 17

In the garden, as in the rest of life, too much of a good thing can be as bad as not enough. Plant roots need oxygen just as we do. If soil is overly saturated, the oxygen is forced out and plants basically drown. **Symptoms of overwatering** include frequent wilting, pale color, root decay, leaf dropping, and an overall lack of vigor.

The same goes for fertilizer: over-fertilizing imparts to plants more nitrogen than they know what to do with. And that, in turn, can cause them to grow weirdly and attract predators.

Conversely, plants with spindly stems and oversized leaves aren't getting enough light.

June 18
Blister Beetles

Short-winged blister beetles, which resemble giant blue ants, often gather in gardens *en masse* during the month of June, to devour the leaves of potatoes and legumes. The shiny, blue-black, short-winged blister beetle is unique in several ways, the least of which is that it has a neck—a rarity in the mostly neckless insect kingdom. It also undergoes myriad metamorphoses, hitches rides on bees, and exudes a caustic chemical called cantharidin, which can burn human skin and kill cattle and horses.

June 19

Shred spare seedlings and damaged leaves around the perimeter of healthy plants to sacrifice to slugs and snails, which go for wilting foliage first.

June 20
Summer Solstice

At the Summer Solstice, the Northern Hemisphere is tilted so that the sun is at its apex in our sky, giving us the year's most direct energy.

If Earth weren't tilted on its axis, we'd have no seasons; the entire globe would get the same amount of sunlight every day of the year.

June 21

The rose, which originated in Arabia, was long associated with Aphrodite, goddess

of love, but later came to symbolize the Virgin Mary. Therefore, the Catholic rosary is organized in multiples of five to represent the fivefold petals of the rose.

June 22

STINK BUGS SUCK.

Some suck the vascular sap from plants; others siphon the vital juices from fellow insects. It is the sap-sucking stink bug's propensity for citrus that inspired one of the earliest recorded uses of biological pest control: in the 13th century, Chinese farmers placed nests of stink bug-eating weaver ants in citrus and litchi trees.

On the flip side of the good stink bug/bad stink bug family tree are the beneficial spined soldier bug and brochymenas, both of which feed on caterpillars, sawfly larvae and leaf beetle grubs.

Stink bugs are slow-moving, shield-shaped, medium-sized bugs, ranging from $1/4$ to $3/4$ inch long. Most are vegetation colored and sport five segmented antenna and many-veined forewings. Though adult stink bugs are capable of flight, they rarely depart terra firma, relying on coloration and their distinctive stink to protect them from predators.

The stink is produced in large paired glands lining the thorax, which pop out when the stink bug is bugged. A concoction of over a dozen vile-smelling chemicals, it effectively repels all but the most determined of predators.

Shiny, spiny, keg-shaped stink bug eggs are laid in fall in small honeycomb-shaped masses attached to leaf surfaces. The nymphs, which resemble miniature adults, hatch in spring.

June 23

Bees in flight build up an electrostatic charge that discharges when they land on grounded flowers, spreading the pollen they're carrying.

For well over a thousand years, little was known about the life cycle of bees: **Aristotle** believed that bee larvae could be harvested from flowering olive trees, and in the 7th century, **St. Isadore of Seville** declared that bees were spontaneously generated from decomposed veal.

June 24 The ancient Greeks originally named the five visible planets—Mercury, Venus, Mars, Jupiter and Saturn—according to their brightness and color. Brilliant white Venus was, for example, Phosphoros, "the light-bearing one," and orange-red Mars, Pyroeis, "the fiery one."

June 25

Ants hear with their knees, picking up vibrations thrumming through the ground.

June 26

Mint gets its name from the Greek nymph Minthe, who tried to seduce Pluto, god of the underworld. When Pluto's wife, Persephone, found out, she turned the little hussy into a fuzzy plant.

June 27

The easiest way to tell a butterfly from a moth is to check the antennae: butterfly antennae are usually straight and slightly thicker at the top, while moths have feathery or bristly ones.

June 28

Many male butterflies and moths spend much of their brief lives sucking down enormous quantities of water and then expelling it from their behinds. Called **puddling**, it's a means of extracting sodium from the water, which they later bestow on females during mating. The females, in turn, donate the prized ion to their offspring.

Male *Gluphisia* moths can take in and spurt out 20 jets of water per minute, each nearly a foot in length. To perform an equivalent feat, a human would have to consume and expel 45,500 quarts of water, at a rate of 3.8 quarts per second, and blow it out his or her rear with the force of a fire hose.

June 29

Some plants do better in a social setting, while others prefer a more solitary life. Many trees, particularly tropical ones, prefer to grow away from their own kind, likely to avoid species-specific, soil-dwelling microbes. Sagebrushes, on the other hand, chemically communicate with one another and work in unison to fend off caterpillars and grasshoppers.

June 30

Ssssexy Ssssnakes

Male snakes are good at foreplay. To get her in the mood, the male runs his tongue along the female's back, rubs his chin against her body, then twines himself around her and sets off a string of rippling muscle contractions.

July 1

This hot, sweet month is named for Julius Caesar, first ruler of the Roman Empire and father of the modern calendar. It's the month of the Full Thunder Moon (due to the frequency of July thunderstorms) or Full Hay Moon (when farmers often cut and bale first-crop hay).

July 2

Step outside tonight and look for constellations. Facing south and looking roughly clockwise from the zenith (directly above), you'll see Corona Borealis, Serpens, Virgo, Libra, Lupus, Scorpius, Sagittarius, and Aquila. Facing north, you can see Hercules, Lyra, Cygnus, Lacerta, Cassiopeia, Perseus, Ursa Major, and Boötes.

July 3

Porcupines sharpen their teeth on rocks.

July 4

The dog days of summer begin. The hottest, most humid part of the summer coincides with the heliacal (just before sunrise) rising of Sirius, the Dog Star, the brightest star in the sky. The ancient Egyptians believed Sirius caused the Nile to rise and water their crops, so they based their calendar around it.

July 5

CUCUMBERS

Cucumbers originated in the eastern Himalayas, but cultivation quickly spread around the globe. The ancient Romans supposedly used cucumbers to treat scorpion bites, bad eyesight and infertility, and to scare

away mice. The emperor Tiberius's fetish for cucumbers spawned a Roman fad of encasing the young fruits in wood, wicker or clay casts to force them to grow in strange and interesting shapes.

July 6

In areas where a good blood meal is hard to come by, such as the Mojave Desert, a **tick** can live up eighteen years without food. In regions where the living is easy, such as the American Midwest, three to five years is the max. While waiting for a passing mammal, a tick will go in and out of a near-hibernation state, reactivating at the first whiff of carbon monoxide. Since it can't fly, it must launch itself onto any passing mammal and quickly scuttle beneath hair or fur. It then buries its mouthparts into the skin and, much like a mosquito, injects an anesthetic and an anticoagulant. Unlike a mosquito, though, it stays on board for days or even weeks, its body bloating exponentially. When it's too full to drink any more, it detaches and falls to the ground.

July 7

Don't worry if plants wilt during the afternoon; it's perfectly normal. In hot weather, plants can't pick up enough moisture to replace the water lost through their leaves, no matter how wet the soil is. Wilting is simply an adaptation; drooping or curling leaves catch less sun and also transpire (lose water to evaporation, which also pulls more water up through the stems) less.

July 8

Katydids

Katydids have ears in their legs, a pair to each set. When they hear something interesting, they raise their forelegs to hear it better.

In Germany, through the 18th and 19th centuries, katydids were popular pets, and street vendors sold small, colorful houses for them.

July 9

When a frog eats something disagreeable, it disgorges its entire stomach, daintily brushes out the offending victual; and stuffs its stomach back down its throat with its front leg that is slightly longer than the other just for that purpose.

July 10

Bars of **soap** hanging from trees will protect an area of about a square meter from garden-munching deer. Commercial repellents containing putrescent (foul-smelling) egg solids are also fairly effective.

July 11

Convinced that the sun fell exhausted every night and needed human blood to give it the strength to rise again the next morning, the Aztecs sacrificed 15,000 men each year to the sun god Huitzilopochtli.

July 12

The word *virga* is derived from the Latin for "twig" or "branch." In meteorology, virga is a streak or shaft of precipitation that evaporates before it hits the ground. It's particularly common in the deserts of the American Southwest but also occurs at high altitudes. Though virga is just a tease, it can be a catalyst for real precipitation by seeding storm cells and helping to create thunderheads.

July 13

Virga occurs on planets other than Earth. On Venus, it is sulfuric acid that evaporates before it reaches the ground; on Mars, it's ice.

July 14

Insects "smell" odors electronically by tuning in to the narrow-band infrared radiation emitted both by other insects and by the plants they consume. Unhealthy plants signal the news of their impending death to waiting insects via this infrared communiqué.

July 15

Peppermint
planted by the back door discourages flies from making your house their home.

July 16

Moths may be drab in color, but they are anything but boring. Some practice virgin birth; others are wildly promiscuous. One species eats only antlers; others slurp grape juice, blood, or cow tears exclusively. No sane bird would lay beak on the cyanide-spraying species, and various other moths carry stink bombs so foul that spiders cut them out of their webs to get rid of the stench. Some merely send out ultrasonic signals saying they taste disgusting, saving themselves the effort of actually doing so. Many moths go through stages where they look like something else, including bird droppings, bumblebees, hornets, oak twigs, and leaves.

July 17

Plants that are pollinated by moths, such as campion, red valerian, sedum and nicotiana, emit a strong scent only at dusk, because most moth pollinators, including hawk moths, are crepuscular (active at twilight) or nocturnal (active at night).

July 18

Mummies from the Iron Age indicate that early humans dined on around 66 different plants, which is more than twice as many varieties as the average American consumes today.

July 19

The Slug

An upside-down melon rind appeals to slugs and draws them away from plants. In a couple of days, you can toss the rind away, along with a bunch of slugs. Damp, rolled-up newspaper works, too, and also snags earwigs.

July 20

Anise is a frilly, licorice-flavored, slow-growing member of the parsley family. Its seeds were once considered so valu-

able that they were used to pay taxes. Humans, dogs, horses, cows, rodents, insects, birds and even fish enjoy the toothsome fruit (which we call seeds). Dogs are particularly fond of it; in fact, it acts as a kind of dog nip. The lure used in greyhound racing is a fake rabbit soaked in anise oil, and foxhounds are encouraged to hunt by chasing after anise-soaked sacks being dragged in front of them.

July 21

Most **insect stings and bites** contain a large amount of acid, so remedies high in alkalis, such as baking soda, help. Wasp and hornet stings, on the other hand, release alkali into the skin, so should be treated with something acidic, like lemon juice or vinegar.

July 22

If pets or wild animals are using your garden as smorgasbord (or a bathroom), a border of lovely, lacy, potent-smelling rue will keep them away. **Rue** is a perennial herb with a bitter taste and blister-raising sap. Be careful when handling rue (wear gloves and long sleeves), and don't plant it if you have young children or pets that might chew it. Rue also has an adverse effect on basil and sage, so plant it well away from them. In European mythology, rue was the only plant not scorched by the breath of the mighty basilisk, the king of evil serpents.

July 23

Male grasshoppers sing to defend their territory. If that doesn't work, they start comparing body parts, like their chunky thighs. If things get really ugly, they'll wrestle, kick and bite.

July 24

More North Americans are allergic to **poison ivy** than any other substance. Poison ivy gets its itch from a chemical called urushiol, which is so durable that people have been known to have severe reactions from handling wood from a tree that had poison ivy growing on it up to fifty years before.

Poison ivy is quite a lovely plant that bears plump, white, bird-pleasing berries. A traditional rhyme for identifying poison ivy warns, "Leaflets three, turn and flee."

July 25

Chickens can see **infrared**. That could be why roosters tend to crow at least 45 minutes before humans can detect light.

July 26

Aphids don't like garlic. If you have aphid-afflicted potted plants, peel a couple of cloves, cut them in half, and bury them just below soil level.

July 27 **Female aphids** are so prolific that they don't even require males. In a process called parthenogenesis, they give live birth to miniature versions of themselves, some of which later morph into males.

The 18th-century French naturalist Reaumur, who clearly had too much time on his hands, calculated that if all the descendants of a single aphid survived a summer and were arranged four abreast in French military formation, their line would extend for 27,950 miles, exceeding the circumference of the earth at the equator!

July 28

THE LONG-TONGUED
WOODPECKER

Woodpecker tongues are crazy long. They attach to the bird's jawbone, run up through one nostril and completely over and around the back of the head, and finally reenter the beak from below. They're coated with sticky saliva, too, to help extract tasty bugs from tree holes.

July 29

Our moon is likely the result of a Mars-sized object colliding with Earth soon after the formation of our solar system. The impact caused the object, along with part of Earth's crust and mantle, to disintegrate and later recombine to form the moon. Proof? Crustal and mantle materials from Earth found in moon rocks.

July 30

Dragonflies

July is prime dragonfly watching time. Male dragonflies are extremely territorial and randy. They spend most of their time threatening each other and preening for passing females, who engage in sultry "Lolita flights" through their territory. Any male that can hold prime mating territory becomes a super stud, impregnating dozens of females. First, though, he has to have sex with himself, to transfer sperm from a storage container at the tip of the abdomen to the copulatory complex near the thorax. That accomplished, he latches onto the back of the current female's head with his rear tow-truck apparatus, and she wraps her legs around his hind end and bends under him in a loop until her hind end connects at his midsection.

The male's organ is equipped with a Swiss army knife–like

unit, and pre-copulation, he performs a quick dilation and curettage to root out any other male's sperm. Afterwards, he literally drags the female around with him to prevent others from barging in, and then hovers possessively overhead while she lays her eggs inside the tissues of aquatic plants, such as bullrushes, cattail, bladderworts and pond lilies.

Dragonflies go through a one-to-three-year underwater larval stage, during which they get around utilizing a unique form of anal jet propulsion. The larvae have a big, hinged, moveable lip, able to shoot out in 100th of a second and seize tadpoles, fish and mosquitoes. When the time comes, the larva climbs out of the water, splits down the back, pumps itself up until it is triple in size, and becomes a shiny new dragonfly.

July 31

Relative to body weight, a hummingbird's brain is bigger than ours. To stay alive, hummingbirds need to eat $1\frac{1}{2}$ to 3 times their weight in insects and nectar every day.

Nectar is a poor source of nutrients, so hummingbirds supplement their liquid diet with regular helpings of spiders and insects, which provide essential amino acids, proteins, vitamins and minerals.

August 1

August was named for Augustus Caesar, first emperor of the Roman Empire and grand-nephew of Julius Caesar. It's the month of the Full Red Moon or Full Green Corn Moon.

Today is **Summer Cross Quarter Day**, the midpoint between the Summer Solstice and Autumnal Equinox.

August 2

The Aztec war god was a hummingbird named Huitzilopochtli, meaning "shining one with a weapon like a cactus thorn."

August 3

The **tomato**
originated on the
slopes of the Andes
as a marble-sized,
fuzzy berry with
smelly foliage. First
cultivated by the
native Nahu people
of Central America,

it was pilfered and taken back to Europe by early Spanish
and Portuguese explorers. There it languished, unloved and
uneaten (and called *wolf peach* and *mala insana*) until discovered by the Italians, who seized upon the luscious round orb,
giving it not only a new name (*pomo amoris,* or love apple) but
a fresh culinary lease on life. There are more than 3,000 varieties of tomatoes today, and at least that many ways to eat,
cook and preserve them.

August 4
To speed up the ripening of your
tomatoes, distract slugs and
snails, and mystify your neighbors, hang a banana from
the stem of your tomato plants. As the banana ripens,
it gives off ethylene, which in turn causes the tomatoes
to ripen. And slugs and snails love bananas even more
than they do tomatoes.

August 5

When the male honeybee ejaculates, his body explodes, leaving behind only his genitals, which remain inside the female. Be glad you're not a male honeybee.

August 6

Tonight's constellations, positioned roughly clockwise from the zenith in the north are Lyra, Cygnus, Lacerta, Pegasus, Andromeda, Pieces, Cassiopeia, Triangulum, Perseus, Ursa Major and Botes. In the south, look for Hercules, Serpens, Ophiuchus, Libra, Scorpius, Sagittarius, Capricornus, and Aquarius.

August 7

Yikes! Guys using outhouses receive the majority of black widow bites. Female black widows often weave their webs just beneath the hole in the seat, and attack guys' dangly bits in defense.

August 8

Sunflowers extract toxins from the soil, including arsenic, lead and uranium, and were used extensively for bioremediation around Chernobyl.

August 9

There are day-biting and night-biting **mosquitoes**, each with appropriate sensors. Day-biters have big eyes and seek their victims by sight, while night-biters pinpoint mammals via their exhaled carbon dioxide streams. Both share the same efficient phlebotomy (Greek for "vein cutting") equipment. Alighting on her (only female mosquitoes drink blood) prey with great delicacy, she pierces the flesh to a depth of half a millimeter with a neat bundle of stylets containing two tubes, two lancets, and two serrated knives. If she's lucky, she'll encounter a vein, and it will take but a moment to consume four times her weight in blood. Otherwise, she has to saw away at a capillary with her knives, a time-consuming and potentially dangerous activity. Before she begins sucking, she spits an anti-coagulant down the two tubes, which mixes with the blood and prevents it from clotting halfway up. This anti-coagulant is the **itch factor** in mosquito bites.

August 10

When a **lightning strike** occurs, the air around it is ionized and superheated to 54,000 degrees F, five times hotter than the Sun. This causes the air to expand so fast that it creates shock waves, which we hear as thunder.

In 1918, Major R. Summerford, a British military officer, was struck by lightning while fighting in Flanders and was temporarily paralyzed from the waist down. He recovered and moved to Vancouver, where, six years later, he was struck again while fishing. Six years after that, he was struck a third time and died. Four years later, his tombstone was destroyed by lightning.

August 11

The **Dog Days of Summer** end today. The Dog Days begin July 3, as Sirius, the Dog Star, starts rising and setting at the same time as the sun. In early Roman times, a brown dog was sacrificed at the beginning of the Dog Days to appease Sirius, who was blamed for the hot, sultry weather.

August 12

The **Perseid meteor shower**—made up of remnants of Comet Swift-Tuttle, first spotted in 1862 and still orbiting the earth—peaks tonight.

August 13

Chiles were likely the first spice used in the Americas; early cooks started using them around 6,000 years ago. If you like your chiles **hot**, let the ground dry out before you pick them; for milder pods, pick right after you water.

August 14

What do you call them? Roly-polies? Sows, pills, armadillos, or potato bugs? Those cute little critters that roll into a ball when threatened are actually woodlice, in the genus *Armadillidium*.

Woodlice are crustaceans and require moisture to both breathe and breed. Females carry their eggs in a side pocket of water, called a marsupium, out of which the babies eventually crawl. Woodlice feed on algae, bark, moss and other decaying organic matter and pose no threat to living plants.

August 15

Ragweed launches 1.6 billion pollen grains per hour. Wind-pollinated plants don't have to design alluring colors or create nectar as bait for insects; they just flood the neighborhood with seed.

August 16

WATER STRIDERS,

also called Jesus bugs, feed on mosquito larvae that float up to the water's surface—and on pretty much anything else that happens to fall into the water (except box elder bugs, which nobody eats). Water striders' stylets secrete an enzyme that dissolves the insides of their victims into a succulent soup, which they then daintily sip.

August 17

Quit watering melons eight to ten days before you harvest to concentrate the sugars.

August 18

In temperate climes, it's time again to start planting cool-weather crops, including beets, beans, carrots, endive, garlic, lettuce, peas, radishes, and spinach. Plant peas and greens between or beneath already established crops for shade.

August 19

Grasshoppers sing their loudest at 95 degrees Fahrenheit and can't sing if it's less than 62 degrees.

If you and a grasshopper were watching a movie together, you would see a continuously moving picture, while your six-legged buddy would see a stream of individual still photos.

August 20

Corn is ripe when the husk is tight and the silk has dried and turned brown.

Early non-Native American farmers, for whom corn (properly called *maize*) was a major staple, often suffered from a form of malnutrition. It was eventually discovered that the indigenous Americans soaked their corn in alkali water, made with ashes, which liberated the niacin in the corn, the lack of which was the underlying cause of the condition known as pellagra.

August 21

Should you see small clouds of **flying ants**, throw some rice and wave your hanky; you're attending an **ant wedding!**

Ant weddings are the synchronized nuptial flights of queen ants and their courts, and they generally occur on hot, humid, windless late-summer days. The winged virgin queens, along with their accompanying males, fly anywhere from a few feet to many miles to mate with ants of the same species from other colonies.

The queens usually mate with several males (who die shortly thereafter), storing their sperm in an abdominal compartment called a spermatheca. Each queen then drops to the ground, sheds her wings, and excavates a new nest. Once settled in, she begins fertilizing her eggs with sperm parsed out of the spermatheca. Queen ants can live as long as 20 years and fertilize millions of eggs, all with the sperm received during the nuptial flight.

August 22

Some species of ants, when alarmed, produce a stinging chemical called formic acid to deter enemies. Unfortunately for the ants, crows and magpies apparently enjoy the effects of formic acid, and so wallow in anthills, avidly rubbing their bodies with the drug-emitting denizens. Scientists speculate that formic acid produces a buzz in the birds similar to that provided by cocaine.

August 23

The American bullfrog's song carries well because it uses its ears as amplifiers.

August 24

Corn plants, one of the favorite foods of the cottonworm moth larva, release a chemical distress signal when eaten by the caterpillars. The chemicals attract adult female parasitic wasps, which lay their eggs in the posterior of the caterpillar. When the wasp eggs hatch, the larva burrow into the caterpillar and eat its insides.

August 25

Wasps, like soldiers, rank each other by their stripes. The yellow and black stripes on their abdomens, combined with colored blotches on their faces, indicate their place in the hierarchy of the nest. Wasps also coat themselves with wax from their home nest to prove where they come from. If they leave and return without the proper wax coating, they're driven away.

August 26

Crows

American crows are found in nearly every habitat across North America, excluding the temperate regions of the Pacific Northwest, where they are supplanted by the common raven.

Omnivorous, opportunistic and extremely intelligent, crows can count, pick individual humans out of a crowd, are self-aware (they recognize themselves in mirrors), and manufacture, modify, and use tools. In cities, they drop hard-shelled nuts onto streets and wait patiently—at crosswalks—for passing cars to crack them open. They cut knives from stiff twigs, or modify wood or wire to spear tasty morsels. Wild hooded crows in Israel have even learned to use breadcrumbs to bait fish.

August 27

The bumble flower beetle, which resembles a hairy June bug, is a true Dionysian: gregarious, benign, and a lover of fermentation. In late summer, large gatherings of these hirsute inebriates can be found copping a buzz from the natural alcohol produced by rotting fruits and vegetables.

August 28 You can harvest just a chunk of cabbage at a time and cover the remainder with plastic or foil. Or you can chop off the entire head, cut a cross in the stem, and get another crop of small heads.

August 29

PRAYING MANTIS

For many years it was thought that praying mantises were deaf because scientists couldn't find their ears. A single ear, located on the underside of the mantis's body, was eventually located. The ear, about a millimeter in length, is recessed and contains two teardrop-shaped eardrums.

Surrealist painter Salvador Dali feared and loathed praying mantises, the females of which often eat their mate mid-copulation, as they personified his fears of castration by women.

August 30

As the barometric pressure drops, plants shift their sugars from leaves and stems to the roots, so crops picked just before a storm are not only less sweet but also less nutritious.

August 31

As many as 10 million bacteria and other microbes live in a single tea-spoonful of soil. A growing body of evidence suggests that all life is the offspring of bacteria, that we are all recombinations of their metabolic processes.

September 1

Septem is Latin for seven, as this was once the seventh month of the year. Native American names include Full Corn and Full Barley Moon.

September 2

Find these constellations:
Facing north, in roughly clockwise order from the zenith, you'll see Cygnus, Lacerta, Pegasus, Andromeda, Triangulum, Boötes, Draco, Hercules and Lyra.

Face south and see Serpens, Aquila, Scorpius, Sagittarius, Capricornus, Aquarius and Pisces.

September 3

Monarchs

Say bye-bye to Monarch butterflies, as they begin their winter migration. Despite their delicate appearance and breezy style of flight, they average about **50 miles per day**. The two major populations of monarch butterflies in North America are separated by the Rocky Mountains. The western group over-winters in coastal California; the eastern in the Transvolcanic Mountains in the Mexican state of Michoacan, at altitudes of up to 11,000 feet.

September 4 It's time to harvest herbs, including aniseed, coriander, dill, echinacea, fennel, garlic, horehound, lavender, oregano, parsley, peppermint, rosehips, rosemary, thyme, valerian, and yarrow. Harvest early in the morning, when plants are at the peak of their flavor.

September 5

Dry herbs by hanging them upside down in bunches or laying them out on a screen. You can also freeze them in ice cube trays or plastic bags.

September 6

This month's birth flower, the aster, is named for Astraea, the goddess of innocence. According to Greek myth, Astraea encountered so much sin among mortals that she metamorphosed into the constellation Virgo to get away from them.

September 7

After Earth, **Mercury** is the
second-densest major
body in the solar sys-
tem. Like Earth, it has
a large, partially molten
iron core and a rocky
mantle beneath its crust.
Mercury's surface is more
like our moon, though, with

cratered terrain and smooth plains, and it appears
to be covered by a thin layer of silicates.

September 8

The word *hurricane* comes from Hurakán, a cranky,
one-legged Mayan deity that was particularly irritable in
late summer and fall. Most Atlantic hurricanes are born
off the western coast of Africa when warm ocean water
evaporates and rises into the windy upper atmosphere,
creating a powerful, spiraling storm with a heated core.
Too bad we can't harness all that power: a typical hurricane releases up to 600 trillion watts of heat energy.

September 9

A RAW,
RIPE

APPLE

is very nearly a perfect food, taking only 85 minutes to completely digest and providing about 40 calories of readily accessible energy. Its chief dietetic value lies in the acids contained in and just below the skin, which aid in the digestion of rich and fatty foods. Apples also contain **antioxidants**, which boost immune function and hinder heart disease and some cancers.

September 10

Agriculturally, the apple (a native of Kazakhstan), is an anomaly or, in botanical terms, a heterozygosity. This means that every seed in every apple contains the genetic plan for a completely new and different tree—most of them, in the words of Thoreau, "sour enough to set a squirrel's teeth on edge." The only way to maintain a specific tree's lineage is to graft it, which is what the Chinese began doing with favored cultivars in 200 B.C.

Discovering a tree with edible fruit was a sure route to fortune and fame during the Great American Apple Rush of the 1800s. Thanks to Johnny Appleseed, apple trees were as common as crows on the American frontier, so the odds of finding a sweet-tasting fruit were around 80,000 to 1. "Every wild apple shrub excites our expectations thus, somewhat as every wild child. It is, perhaps, a prince in disguise," exclaimed Thoreau. When an edible apple was discovered, the tree was treated much like a Triple Crown—winning stud horse. In 1914, the single Golden Delicious tree from whence all subsequent Golden Delicious trees have come, was sold for $5,000 and padlocked inside a steel cage wired with an alarm.

September 11

In cool climes, **songbirds** are flocking together in anticipation of migration. Many migrating songbirds fly at night to avoid overheating and predation. It is believed that they use the moon and stars to guide them, as well as magnetic cues and visual landmarks. Ornithologists often count migrating birds by the light of the autumnal full moon; one Colorado researcher counted more than 9,000 birds on a single September night.

September 12

Listen: the **crickets are getting louder**. As fall progresses, mating becomes imperative, as adult crickets perish come winter. The loud, monotonous song we hear in the evening is that of the males, singing to attract a mate; they sing a quicker, softer song when a female approaches. There's also a territorial tune, sung when two males meet, and an abrupt "Look out!" chirp that warns everyone to be quiet.

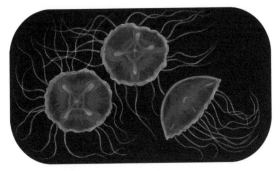

September 13

Craspedacusta, the freshwater jellyfish, probably hitchhiked (it certainly has the arms) from its native China via water lilies sometime in the late 1800s and has since infiltrated temperate waterways across the country. Quarter-sized, harmless (except to plankton) and rarely seen, freshwater jellyfish sometimes "bloom" in early fall, filling lakes and ponds with thousands of tiny floating pseudo-medusae.

September 14

The roadrunner really is fast, crafty, quirky and fearless, and pretty much the coolest, most personable bird in North America. A fearsome predator, the roadrunner feeds on snakes (including rattlesnakes), lizards, scorpions, insects, rodents and other birds, though it also enjoys hotdogs, dog food and lunchmeat, as many residents of the Southwest can attest. It's not uncommon for a roadrunner to make the rounds of homes in its territory, tapping on windows to announce its arrival and waiting expectantly for a handout.

September 15

Though it can fly plenty fast, the roadrunner prefers to chase prey on foot, commonly reaching speeds of 17 to 20 mph. Seizing its prey with its long, sharp beak, the roadrunner then slams it against a tree, a telephone pole or the ground until it's not only long dead but also long and pulpy. The roadrunner then swallows it whole, like a snake, an inch or two at a time; so you often see a roadrunner roaming about with a portion of snake dangling from its mouth.

September 16

If you want to avoid biting black flies, just don't breathe. The female of many black fly species requires a protein found in blood in order to form and lay eggs; so when she's feeling maternal, she samples the breeze for excess carbon dioxide, a sure sign of animal respiration. Following the breath trail, she tracks her victim, and once within 15 to 20 feet, switches to visual mode and hones in on a landing site. Male black flies, on the other hand, are vegetarians, feeding exclusively on nectar.

September 17

Mercury travels around the Sun in a mere 88 days but takes 59 Earth days to rotate on its axis. This strange combination results in a single day on Mercury lasting 176 Earth days.

September 18

Because of its small mass, gravity on Mercury is only about a third of that on Earth, so an object weighing 100 pounds here would weigh only about 38 pounds there.

September 19

In temperate zones, now's the time to divide and transplant bleeding heart, daylily, delphinium, forget-me-not, lily of the valley, peony, phlox and

primrose, and to dig up tender bulbs such as gladiola. Cure the bulbs in the sun for a few days, then wrap them in newspaper and store in a cool, dark place.

September 20

The *banana slug*, which indeed resembles a large, over-ripe banana (sometimes a green, brown or white one), is a native of the Pacific coastal coniferous rainforest. A world-class composter, it has a raspy tongue with 27,000 teeth and a particular fondness for mushrooms and feces. It oozes along at the fairly rapid clip (for a slug) of three to four inches a minute, leaving behind a trail of nitrogen-rich fertilizer.

To avoid having their mouths glued together by slime, the banana slug's predators (raccoons, shrews, ducks, geese and moles) roll the slug in dirt before dining.

September 21

Tree squirrels eat acorns, bark, berries, flowers, tree sap and nuts, as well as bird eggs and baby birds.

September 22
Autumnal Equinox

Today the sun is directly over the equator, and day and night are equal all around the planet. Tomorrow it passes into the Southern Hemisphere, leaving us a little more in the dark every day from now until the Winter Solstice.

September 23

Turnips

Root crops, such as beets, carrots, parsnips, rutabagas and turnips, can be left in the ground through the fall and winter. Once a hard freeze occurs, mulch them over with a heavy layer of straw to keep the ground from freezing.

September 24
LITTLE BROWN BAT

For creatures that sleep nearly 20 hours out of every 24, little brown bats surely do get around. They typically travel between three roosting sites—for day, night and hibernation. When they're not snoozing upside down, little brown bats are hunting and eating—anywhere from 600 to 1,000 moths, mosquitoes, gnats, beetles, midges, mayflies and wasps per bat in a mere 2 to 4 hours. That's a lot of pests munched down, making little brown bats a friend to farmers and mosquito-averse city dwellers alike. Preternaturally agile, they can snatch insects with their teeth or net them with their wings, tossing them from wing to tail to mouth—mid-flight.

Little brown bats are found in all environments, from urban to wild, across most of North America, with populations heaviest in the northern United States and southern Canada. They mate in mid- to late autumn while swarming near hibernation spots, then retire *en masse* until insects begin hatching again in mid-spring. Most females give birth to a single pup each year and nurse it for approximately three weeks. Bats are among the few species of mammals that will care for each other's young and bring food to sick or disabled roost mates.

September 25

Cultivate delayed gratification: plant crocus, daffodils, grape hyacinth, iris, narcissus, scillas, snowdrops and tulips now. Come next spring, you'll be glad you did.

You can plant bulbs in large containers; miniature daffodils, grape hyacinth and crocus work well.

September 26

Cautious male praying mantises may take up to an hour to travel a single foot toward a hungry, horny female. Though if he slips up, he'll still get to mate, since that doesn't require a head.

September 27

Give outdoor chrysan-themums a sprinkle of Epsom salts; they'll appreciate the magne-sium. Potted ones will too.

September 28

Goose, eh?

Is there another sound in the natural world that so catches in the throat and heart as the call of the Canada goose?

The **Canada goose** is the most common goose in North America, easily recognized by its poignant honk and V-shaped flock formation. It is chiefly a grazer, feeding on marsh vegetation and field crops like corn and wheat.

Its wild range is vast, stretching from the Aleutian Islands south throughout the United States. In many urban areas, Canada geese are year-round residents, nesting on the edges of ponds and streams at night and commuting to rural areas to feed on field stubble during the day.

Canada geese are intensely loyal to flock and family members. While traveling, if an individual goose gets sick or is wounded, two additional geese drop out of formation and follow it down to protect it. They stay until the afflicted goose either dies or is able to fly again.

September 29

Plant and transplant deciduous bushes and trees only after their foliage has started to change color. Don't fertilize new trees until their second year; they need time to establish roots.

September 30

Plants everywhere are maturing and sending their seeds out into the world to create next season's crops. Some seeds float on wings or parachutes; some drift along with the breeze.

Others have tiny hooks or spikes to attach to animal fur or pant legs; still others explode from their pods like little grenades; and many, with their succulent surrounding flesh, entice birds or animals to eat and excrete them or bury them in the ground.

October 1

October takes its name from the Latin *octo,* or eight, for on the old Roman calendar, this was the eighth month of the year. Some early Native American tribes called this the month of the Full Travel Moon or the Full Dying Grass Moon.

October 2

You can dig up **rosemary, basil, tarragon, oregano, marjoram, English thyme, parsley,** and **chives** to grow inside for the winter. Keep in a cool, sunny spot, and let the soil completely dry before watering.

October 3

In the north sky tonight, looking roughly clockwise from the zenith, you'll see Pegasus, Andromeda, Triangulum, Cassiopeia, Perseus, Auriga, Ursa Major, Ursa Minor, Boötes, Draco, Hercules, Lyra, and Cygnus. In the south sky are Aquila, Serpens, Sagittarius, Corona Australis, Indus, Cetus, Aquarius, Pisces, and Lacerta. Deep in the sky, the Andromeda galaxy is visible.

October 4

If you encounter an

opossum,

try hard not to scare it. When
opossums play possum—which
they do when frightened and
unable to flee—they not only enter
into an involuntary shock-like state
resembling death, but also discharge a
rank-smelling greenish substance from their anal glands.

In size and appearance, the opossum falls somewhere
between a cat, a rat and a pig, having paper-thin ears, pink
feet, a long, prehensile tail, and a bulbous pink nose at the
end of a pointy snout. It also has thumbs on its hind feet.
Intelligence-wise, opossums beat dogs paws down, their intel-
lect being more on the level of swine.

October 5

Leave garden soil bare for a few weeks before spreading
winter mulch or planting cover crops. This will give the
birds time to dig through the soil and eat pests and their
eggs. In a couple of weeks, lay down a layer of chopped
leaves or other mulch, or plant winter rye, crimson clover,
or hairy vetch, to reduce erosion and nutrient leaching.

October 6 **Mottephobia** is a fear

of moths. It was long believed that
moths were the souls of the dead flinging themselves against
the windows of the living.

October 7

In cold climates,
California quail
are beginning to band
together. Quick-footed
little families merge
into boisterous coveys of
bobbing heads and flashing
wings. In the wild, as many as
200 quail may flock for the
winter season; in urban areas, most groups number in
the teens. This time of year they feed on the seeds of
clover, lupine, vetch and grass as well as grapes, acorns
and berries.

October 8

Brown trout are spawning. Elk, white-tailed
deer and pronghorn are in rut. Moose are
making big love. Porcupines are doing it very,
very carefully.

October 9

October is a magical time to study the heavens; the sky is clear, the air is brisk, the Milky Way is clearly visible, and all the planets are coming back into view. Plus, the nights are getting longer; sunset comes two minutes earlier each evening this month.

October 10

It's time to plant evergreens, garlic, lilies, rhubarb, roses, shallots, spring bulbs, trees and shrubs.

acorn

chokecherry

hazel catkins

Consider planting trees and shrubs that provide winter food and shelter for wildlife— e.g., birch, chokecherry, crabapple, cranberry, dogwood, juniper, hawthorn, holly, oak, pine, snowberry, sumac, willow and winterberry.

October 11

Fall **cankerworms** are emerging from their cocoons as adult moths eager to mate. The dull gray, wingless females climb tree trunks to await the winged, striped males and then lay clusters of barrel-shaped eggs, which will hatch in mid-spring. Fall cankerworm larvae, called inchworms, are a favorite meal of orioles and other migratory songbirds.

October 12

Autumn smells so very delicious, sometimes unexpectedly so. Aside from the nostalgia, the nose-tickling bouquet of fallen leaves and the heady spice of marigolds and mums, you might sniff out yummy, licorice-smelling lavender hyssop leaves, carrot-scented Queen Anne's lace, the sharp turpentine rush of aster leaves, and the freaky pizza scent of wild bergamot seed heads.

October 13

Overseed lawns with Dutch white clover to create a self-fertilizing lawn, choke out weeds, and soften soil. Bacteria around roots of clover actually pull water vapor out of the air. Bees and butterflies like it, too, and it's pretty.

October 14

woolly bear caterpillar's

Legend has it that the wider the

orangey-brown middle band, the milder the impending winter. But the woolly bear's famous prognosticating band is actually an indicator of age: the wider the band, the earlier in the season the woolly bear was hatched. And, as early hatchings indicate a warm and early spring, the woolly bear does indeed wear the weather in its wool, but it's last season's pattern, not the next.

October 15

IT'S
PECAN
HARVESTING TIME!

Pecan comes from the Algonquin word for "nut requiring a stone to crack." Pecan trees are lovely, have wonderful hardwood, and can bear fruit for over 300 years!

Studies indicate that pecans are effective in lowering cholesterol and may prevent age-related nerve degeneration.

October 16

The moon is regularly shaken by small moonquakes, thought to be caused by the gravitational pull of Earth. Sometimes tiny fractures appear at the surface and gas escapes.

October 17

Alfred Hitchcock's **The Birds** was based on a true story. Or at least the original story, written by Daphne du Maurier, was. Forty years after the fact, scientists came to the conclusion that a large group of seagulls went batty from eating anchovies that had eaten toxic algae.

October 18

Indian Summer, a spell of warm weather also known as St. Luke's Little Summer, often occurs now.

October 19

Autumn leaves are a huge gift to
gardeners. With minimal effort, they can be used to
feed plants, build the soil, protect against disease,
shelter tender perennials, and control weeds. And
they're free!

What's important is shredding them. Left whole,
they'll mat together, preventing oxygen and bacteria
from penetrating the layers. The easiest way to shred
them is to simply run over them with the lawn mower a
few times. This is particularly handy if it's the lawn you
want to feed; just mow them into bits and leave them.

Or, if you have a leaf blower, forget the blowing part
and turn it to "vacuum." Your leaves will be nicely shredded, and contained too.

Once they're shredded, you can:

- Feed the soil—Cover garden beds with a 3- to 4-inch
  layer of shredded leaves, or turn them under with
  a tiller.

- Compost them—Leaf mold is a horticultural mainstay
  that can even be used to replace peat in potting
  soil mixes. Whether you're composting them alone
  or adding them to an existing pile, be sure to soak
  them down.

- Use as mulch. Tuck a 4- to 6-inch layer around perennials for winter protection.

October 20

Fifty to 60 million years before humans began cultivating plants for food, several species of ants made the transition from hunter-gatherers to agriculturists, growing their own fungus supplies and managing fungal weed invasions.

October 21

Tonight is the **Orionid meteor shower**. A meteoroid is a small rock in space. If it enters Earth's atmosphere, it's a meteor. If it reaches the ground, it's a meteorite.

October 22

The WOOD STORK, the only stork native to North America, finds food by touch, or tacto-location. When a fish brushes against its highly sensitive beak, the beak snaps shut in about 25 milliseconds, one of the fastest reflexes known in the animal kingdom.

October 23

The discovery of **new microbial life** deep inside the earth has some scientists speculating that there might be a hidden biosphere beneath the surface whose total number of organisms may rival or exceed that on the surface.

October 24

Spiders' brains are so large that they extend into their legs. In some species, the brain occupies up to 80% of the spider's body, and the smaller the spider, the proportionately larger the brain. (Spiderlings often have lumps on their abdomens containing brain mass.) By comparison, human brains represent only 2–3% of our body mass. The spider's gigantic brain is likely necessary for web weaving.

October 25

During the Middle Ages, blackberry bushes were said to be the preferred urinal of the devil. It's time to trim those devil's urinals and other berry canes back to just above soil level.

October 26

Daddy Longlegs

The daddy longlegs spider is really not a spider at all, but rather a phalangid, an order of insects that sports eight outrageously long, slender appendages. Those extensive extensions are kept darned busy, used as they are to fight, fornicate and flee.

When male daddy longlegs pull each other's legs, they aren't fibbing, they're fighting. The aggressor, who positions himself above his opponent, grabs a leg with his jaws, or palpi, and yanks up, down or around in a clockwise direction three to five times. If the leg doesn't break off, they change positions, and keep changing them until one does fall off, and the loser skulks away.

Love is no easier than war, and far more confusing. The male must first sneak up on the female and, using his palpi, grab her body behind her second pair of legs. With his first pair of legs, he then restrains her second pair, and his second pair acts as an early warning system for would-be interlopers or predators. His remaining four legs are used to keep himself upright during the whole complicated encounter, which can take anywhere from seconds to hours, depending on his skill and her cooperation, or lack of. Afterwards, he uses all of his (remaining) legs to form a cage over her, forcing her to oviposit before seeking more adroit lovers.

The daddy longlegs' first line of defense against predators is a foul secretion, which squirts from the base of his second pair of legs. If that doesn't work, however, they "leg it" out of there. If seized in flight, they simply leave the trapped append-age behind and keep on running.

Daddy longlegs are also known as "harvestmen."

October 27

In cold climes, it's time to winterize the pond: pull out annuals; trim back perennials; remove as much gunk as possible; install a floating deicer.

October 28

Rattlesnakes

are slithering together to form communal hibernation knots in burrows and under cliffs. Worms are migrating downward, and frogs and turtles are heading into deeper, colder water because cold water holds more oxygen than warm water.

October 29

White-tailed deer are in rut. Found throughout the United States (except Alaska, California, Nevada, Utah and Hawaii), as well as in Canada, Mexico, and Central and South America, white-tailed deer can live just about anywhere and eat just about anything. Their diet includes clover, grasses, cacti, acorns, mushrooms, field mice and ground-nesting birds. A population of white-tailed deer in upstate New York is entirely white, though not albino.

October 30

Mule deer are forming into herds that will stay together until the Vernal Equinox. The polygamous bucks are perusing the herd for potential mates, and the pugilistic does are sparring among themselves. Mule deer, which are found west of the Missouri River, are quite combative, particularly the does. While the bucks generally battle only during rutting season, the does are contentious most of the year. So throughout spring and summer, mule deer travel in small, segregated groups—a single female with her offspring; males in groups of two or three—and come together only for the fall rut and winter season.

October 31

Today is **Winter Cross-Quarter Day**, the midpoint between the Autumnal Equinox and the Winter Solstice.

A cockroach can live for up to nine days without its head.

November 1

November takes its name from the Latin *novem,* the number nine, as this was once the ninth month of the year. For some early Native American tribes, this was the month of the Full Beaver or Full Frost Moon.

November 2

This month's birth flower, the **chrysanthemum**, was cultivated in China as far back as the 15th century B.C. Some chrysanthemums contain pyrethrum, a natural insecticide that attacks the nervous system of insects and prevents female mosquitoes from biting. Commercial insecticides made from pyrethrum are considered to be among the safest to use around food crops and are less toxic to mammals and birds than synthetic ones, though they are harmful to fish.

People ingesting the psychoactive DMT, found in many plants (and in trace amounts in the human body), often have visual hallucinations of . . . chrysanthemums!

November 3
You can plant spring bulbs, rose bushes, deciduous trees and shrubs until the ground freezes hard.

If you're expecting snow and freezing weather, now is the time to mow the lawn one last time. If you have a gas mower or tiller, drain it. Same goes for the sprinkler system and garden hoses.

And don't forget to give all perennials, trees, and shrubs a thorough watering before the ground freezes hard. Though they may appear dormant, their roots are still actively growing.

November 4
Plutarch, a first-century Greek historian, biographer, essayist and senior priest of Apollo at the Oracle of Delphi, believed that the moon is a way station for arriving and departing souls. One of the moon's impact craters is named for him.

November 5

Constellations in tonight's northern sky: Pegasus, Pisces, Andromeda, Triangulum, Perseus, Taurus, Auriga, Ursa Major, Ursa Minor, Draco, Hercules, and Lyra. In the southern sky are Lacerta, Cygnus, Sagitta, Aquila, Capricornus, Piscis Austrinus, Phoenix, and Cetus.

November 6

FOR MANY

CENTURIES,

people thought that weather occurred in only one place and simply stayed there until it ran out. Benjamin Franklin first suspected this wasn't the case when he learned that a storm he experienced in Philadelphia was followed by a suspiciously similar one in Boston the next night. In Franklin's days, weather predictions were based on the observations of kamikaze balloonists, who went aloft in search of approaching storms (and who often passed out from oxygen deprivation).

November 7

In temperate climes, it's time to **finish cleaning up the garden**. Sigh. Cut back perennials to a few inches above soil level and mulch well with 4 to 5 inches of straw, leaves or compost.

Pull up annuals and compost them away from where you intend to plant next spring. That is, unless they'll provide birds and other animals with winter fodder. In that case, leave them as they are.

November 8
Broccoli

If you're in the Southern Tier, it's time to plant cool-weather vegetables again, including beets, broccoli, cabbage, carrots, kale, lettuce, onions, peas and spinach.

November 9

THE HOUSE MOUSE

originated in Eurasia around 2 million years ago. After assisting many times in the spread of the bubonic plague, it hopped aboard Spanish ships to the New World and set up residence in North, South and Central America in the early 1500s.

House mice are gregarious, living together in small groups and sharing common eating, nesting and bathroom areas. Though they are incredibly prolific (females reproduce at about two months and give birth to litters of 6 to 11 every 21 days), they usually don't overpopulate an area. In fact, when a population grows too dense, many of the females, particularly the adolescents, become infertile.

However, please note the word "usually." In 1926–27, an estimated 82,000 mice per acre chewed, gnawed and shredded their way through Central Valley, California.

Fortunately, unlike its cousins the deer mouse and the white-footed mouse, the house mouse has not been found to be a carrier of hantavirus.

November 10

Hydras
are simple, predatory organisms that live in warm, unpolluted freshwater ponds, lakes and streams, feeding on small aquatic invertebrates. Only a few millimeters long, they lack head and brain but possess thin, stinging tentacles armed with neurotoxins. Hydras are cool and strange in all sorts of ways, but most impressive is this: they constantly regenerate themselves, and therefore never age or die. Hydras are, it seems, immortal.

November 11

Hobo spiders mate in the fall and often come inside as they search for a partner. Medium in size and beige-ish in color, the hobo can be distinguished by a distinctive herringbone pattern on its long, slender body. The more poisonous male sports two dark, fuzzy "boxing gloves"—actually his genitalia—at the end of its pedipalps, or front feelers. The hobo spider is native to Europe and first appeared in Seattle in the 1930s. Since then, it has spread across much of the northwestern United States. As a non-native, the hobo has no natural enemies, though jumping spiders often kill them. So if you live in hobo spider territory, make friends with any resident jumping spiders; as the hobo's enemy, they are very much your friends.

November 12

HUMANS ARE WEIRD

During the Middle Ages, stag beetles were believed to set houses on fire. In 14th-century France, an ecclesiastical hearing was held in which it was announced that any beetle that did not attend the trial would be excommunicated.

November 13

NATURE IS WEIRD

The hairworm parasite, which lives inside grasshoppers, pumps its host full of chemicals that cause the grasshopper to commit suicide by jumping into water, thereby allowing the parasite to swim free and find a new host.

November 14

Perennial herbs, such as rosemary and sage, can be harvested year-round. In Europe, rosemary is associated with memory and is worn at weddings, war commemorations and funerals. As Ophelia says in Hamlet, "There's rosemary, that's for remembrance."

November 15

Conifers, like deciduous trees, shed in the fall. Because the oldest needles are shed, the inner areas of the tree closer to the trunk become less dense than the outer areas. Pine trees usually shed three-year-old needles, whereas spruce and fir shed needles that are four to five years old.

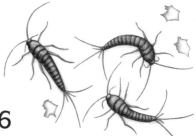

November 16

Silverfish are the greased pigs of the bug world, with soft scales that slip off easily in a predator's grasp. Silverfish feed on book paste, wallpaper, oatmeal, flour, house dust, starch and each other. They engage in long, stately courtships, exchanging erotic messages through antennae and tails.

November 17
Tonight and tomorrow night, look to the south for the Leonid meteor shower. Every 33 years or so, the Leonid shower produces a "meteor storm," with thousands of meteors per hour.

November 18

A bird's beak determines not just its diet but its song, too. Heavy beaks, designed to crush tough seeds or shellfish, make deeper, less complicated sounds than the melodious songs produced by slim bug-snatching beaks.

November 19

Clothes moth larvae

get their B vitamins and minerals by eating fabric stains. According to *Household Book,* published in 1590, a raw goat's liver placed in the closet or cupboard will drive out clothes moths. Pheromone traps, however, are slightly less messy and easier to come by.

November 20

Before pumpkin pie

was invented, people prepared a sweet pumpkin dessert by slicing off the top of the pumpkin, removing the seeds, and filling the insides with milk, spices and honey. The whole thing was then baked in hot ashes.

November 21

The name **cranberry** probably derives from it being a favorite food of cranes, though some sources claim the name comes from "craneberry," because just before the cranberry's flower expands, its stem, calyx and petals resemble the neck, head and bill of a crane.

Cranberry plants are low, creeping dwarf evergreen shrubs and vines that grow in acidic bogs in cool regions. Cranberries are grown commercially in Wisconsin, Massachusetts, Washington, Oregon and New Jersey as well as in much of Canada.

Most cranberries are "wet harvested": the bogs are flooded and the water is stirred up to loosen the berries from the vines. Because they have pockets of air inside, the berries float, and so can be rounded up and lifted out by conveyor or pumped into a truck.

November 22

Proportionally, the stomach of a pig is much smaller than that of a cow or sheep, so overeating would more appropriately be called "cowing out" or "sheeping out."

November 23

In much of the world, **entomophagy, or bug eating**, is common. Grasshoppers, black ant larvae, water bug eggs, moths, grubs, caterpillars, giant water bugs, and locusts are most commonly eaten. One hundred grams of grasshopper contains about 20 grams of protein and 6 grams of fat, as opposed to 24 grams of protein and 18 grams of fat in the same amount of beef. Grasshoppers also contain four times as much calcium and twice as much iron as beef. Yum.

November 24

When cut, onions release sulfuric compounds that, when combined with air, activate a compound called *thiopropanal sulfoxide.* To reduce tears, burn a candle nearby to oxidize it.

November 25

Turkeys are far from stupid.

They are alert, sensitive, and playful. They also appear to have a concept of death and hold turkey wakes for deceased flock members. The Aztecs were the first to domesticate turkeys, originally known as *huexoloti*. Christopher Columbus took the turkey to Spain, and from there it spread to the Middle East, where Turkish farmers perfected breeding turkeys. English settlers, who took the plump Middle Eastern version with them to Jamestown in 1614, were surprised to see the turkey's wild cousins already well established in the New World.

Ben Franklin performed an experiment in which he shocked a turkey in the head, electrocuting it, then revived it "by repeated blowing into its lungs." This is likely the first use of artificial respiration both on a turkey and to treat electrical shock.

November 26

Tooth amoebas, *Entameba gingivalis,* live in the stagnant backwaters of your mouth, feeding on the same food you feed on. Though little is known about these infinitesimal orifice workers, it appears that they do not cause disease and may, in fact, protect us from even less desirable denizens.

November 27

The four most prominent families in ancient Rome named themselves after beans:

Lentulus (lentil),
Fabius (fava),
Cicero (chickpeas),
and Pisos (peas).

November 28

Chickadee

Cute, chunky little black-capped chickadees, with their easily recognized "chick-a-dee-dee-dee" call, are found in all but the most southern regions of the United States (where their cousins the Carolina chickadees fill in). They are year-round regulars at most bird feeders. Chickadees love suet, peanut butter, sunflower seeds and millet, and will take extras to stash for later. Researchers have found that black-capped chickadees living in rugged environments, such as Alaska and northern Montana, have a larger hippocampus (memory area of the brain) than those living in milder regions. That's because those chickadees have to store more food and remember where they hid it.

Chickadees sometimes fake alarm calls to scare other birds away, allowing the chickadees to hog coveted food sources.

November 29

Rats experience REM sleep, which suggests that they dream. They also whistle to each other from deep within their throats and chirp with joy when playing.

November 30

Plants develop ingenious ways to survive winter. Some hide underground as roots, bulbs and tubers crammed with food; some secrete alcohols and sugars as a kind of antifreeze or grow low to the ground to avoid wind chill. Others, such as mountain laurel, grow hairs as insulation, or, like lichens, dehydrate.

December 1

December takes its name from *decem,* the Latin word for ten, for on the original Julian calendar, this was the tenth month. For some early Native American tribes, this was the month of the Full Cold Moon or Full Long Nights Moon.

December 2

Facing north tonight and looking roughly clockwise from the zenith, you'll see Pisces, Triangulum, Perseus, Auriga, Gemini, Ursa Major, Ursa Minor, Hercules, Draco, Lyra, Cygnus, Cepheus, Cassiopeia, and Lacerta. Facing south you can see Andromeda, Pegasus, Aquarius, Capricornus, Piscis Austrinus, Phoenix, Fornax, and Cetus.

Deep in the sky, the Andromeda galaxy and the double star in Cygnus are visible.

December 3

Paperwhite narcissus make a lovely holiday gift, and unlike other bulbs, they don't need a period of cold before being planted or "forced" inside. They take about three weeks to bloom, so this would be a good time to pot some up. Paperwhites look particularly lovely set in a clear container filled with marbles or pretty rocks.

December 4

JUPITER!

Jupiter's core may be as hot as 54,000 degrees Fahrenheit. That heat, produced when Jupiter formed, slowly escapes into space, creating a swirling banner of clouds. Because of Jupiter's rapid rotation, the clouds form bands of different colors, making  Jupiter look like a striped beach ball with a big red spot in its southern hemisphere. The red spot is a hurricane-like storm large enough to swallow two Earths.

December 5

Rats and humans have a lot in common. Both:

- migrated from east to west in the life journey of their species.

- are omnivorous and adaptable to all climes.

- live in well-ordered social groups.

- reproduce regardless of season or food supply;.

- engage in homosexual behavior.

- practice cannibalism.

- frequently engage in warfare among their own kind.

The more you know, the harder it is to separate yourself from the animal kingdom, isn't it?

December 6

In cold areas, many fish—including **bass**, bullheads and carp—are dormant this time of year; some partly bury themselves in muddy lake and river bottoms. Bony fish, including bass, have otoliths, or "fish ear bones," which are used for balance, orientation and sound detection. Made of lovely, ivory-like calcium carbonate concretions, they form in concentric layers about a nucleus, creating an indelible record of the fish's growth rate, much like the rings of a tree.

December 7

Snowflakes are composites of snow crystals that collide on their journey down from the clouds. Snow falling in early winter usually forms the largest and loveliest flakes; later in the season, when temperatures are lower, crystals don't adhere to one another as readily. Crystals formed in colder air are also brittle, so when they collide their arms break off. It's all those tiny, broken spicules that make up late-season snow.

December 8

Some insects with large body cavities freeze solid during the winter. Their insides first turn to slush, which prevents the formation of large ice crystals that would rupture their cells.

* * *

Physicians once used biting insects, such as ants and beetles, to suture wounds. The insect was held to the wound and induced to bite. Once its jaws were clamped in place, its head was pinched off and stayed stuck to the person's flesh until . . . ick.

December 9

Beavers, which stay active all winter, have castor sacs in their stomachs that contain castoreum, a complex substance considered by Hippocrates and other early physicians to have healing properties. Modern research shows that it contains salicylic acid, the active ingredient in aspirin. Castoreum is also used as perfume base. What it does for the beaver, no one knows.

Beavers are said to cry real tears when hurt or frightened. They are also monogamous and mate for life.

December 10

There's an orgy of dust mites in your bed—anywhere between 10,000 and 10,000,000 of them—eating your dead skin and dandruff, fornicating, giving birth, defecating and dying. It's been estimated that 10 percent of the weight of a two-year-old pillow is composed of dead mites and their droppings. Maybe it's time to get a new pillow.

December 11

Poinsettias need six hours of indirect light and a warm room to flourish. Don't let them stand in water.

The Aztecs called the poinsettia *cuetlaxochitl,* meaning "skin flower," and used it both to produce red dye and to reduce fever.

December 12

Fluffy, fresh-fallen snow absorbs sound waves. Conversely, when snow hardens, it reflects sound waves, making even subtle natural sounds easy to hear.

December 13

Tonight is the Geminid meteor shower, usually the best show of the year.

December 14

Halcyon Days, a period of calm weather, often occurs this week. Legend has it that this respite is caused by the halcyon, or **kingfisher**— a large, fish-eating bird that builds a floating nest. The female halcyon is brooding this time of year and is said to charm the wind and waves, enabling her young to safely fledge.

December 15

A female pigeon can't lay eggs if she's alone, or thinks she is. In order for her ovaries to function, she must see another pigeon (though her own reflection in a mirror works).

December 16

They may look messy and random
to you, but those cobwebs in the
corner are actually sophisti-
cated snares assembled by
the master of webs, the
American house spider.

At the base of the trap
are sticky, highly elastic
anchor threads that break
on contact and hoist hapless
victims into a raised web. So
well constructed is the trap, and
so boundless the appetite of its archi-
tect, that on one well-documented occasion, a house mouse
was ensnared and duly sampled.

For one of such imposing skill and gluttony, the American
house spider is rather unprepossessing in appearance. The
female sports a bulbous, yellowish-brown abdomen decorated
with gray and black streaks and has long banded legs. The
smaller male is similar in color through the abdomen, though
his legs are orange, without the stripes.

Unusually gregarious for arachnids, house spider couples
often cohabitate and even share food. After a creepy but non-
fatal courting, the female lays her eggs and wraps them in a
small, brown silk cocoon, which she anchors in a secure corner
of the web. Upon hatching, the young spiderlings mature rap-
idly, leaving the nest after only a few days to go off and weave
impressive constructs of their own.

December 17
For those in the **Southern Tier,** it's time to prune summer- and fall-blooming shrubs and vines, to feed and mulch camellias and azaleas, and to plant roses, California poppies and sweet peas.

December 18
If you were the same size as an ant, you'd be able to lift up to 50 times *your* body weight, too. As an organism becomes smaller, its overall weight drops far more quickly than its strength. Conversely, as organisms get larger, muscle strength increases at a much slower rate.

December 19
It's been discovered that birds can learn foreign languages—or at least nuthatches can learn black-capped chickadee. While it's not unusual for one animal to react to the alarm call of another, nuthatches seem to go beyond that, interpreting the type and level of threat and the predator it's posed by.

December 20

This is mating season for **great horned owls.** Though mostly solitary, each year around the time of the Winter Solstice, they seek out their lifelong mate and spend the long, cold nights of deep winter hunting and roosting as a duo.

The great horned owl is identifiable by its size (nearly two feet tall), prominent, wide-set ear tufts, bright yellow eyes, and porcelain throat. It's found everywhere from woodland to desert, open field to urban park.

Known as the "tiger of the sky," it is powerful enough to take porcupine-size prey. Despite this fearsome rep, however, great horned owls are often tormented during daylight hours by crows, which chase the groggy owls from tree to tree.

December 21
Winter Solstice

In the Northern Hemishpere, today is the shortest day of the year, as the sun reaches its farthest point south. For the next three days, it will rise and set at the same time and then begin its journey back to the Northern Hemisphere.

This was the day when the Druids harvested mistletoe, using a golden sickle reserved for this purpose only.

December 22

American dwarf **mistletoe** is a common parasite that grows on conifers. As its berries ripen, they build hydrostatic pressure and eventually shoot out a single, sticky seed at 50 mph, as far as 50 feet. Once established on a new host, the seed sends out bark-penetrating roots to pirate water and nutrients. Though toxic to humans, mistletoe berries provide high-protein winter fodder for deer and elk.

Mistletoe extract has been shown to kill cancer cells and stimulate the immune system.

December 23 **Boxelder bugs**

overwinter as adults in protected south- and west-facing cracks and crevices and come out to soak up warmth on sunny winter days. While boxelder bugs are often considered a nuisance, they do no harm, at least not beyond leaving streaks of excreta when in large aggregations. Boxelder bugs don't even damage the female boxelder and maples trees they feed upon, as they eat only leaf litter and seedpods. The boxelder bug's distinctive black and orange coloring is a message to predators that they taste bad—and they must, since absolutely nothing eats them.

December 24

Tonight was once celebrated as Mother Night, when all the great goddesses gave birth and the world was born. Animals were believed to possess the gift of speech, and the trees in the forest were said to bloom briefly at midnight, producing fruit that granted immortality.

December 25

Evergreens have long been cherished at this time of year as a symbol of rebirth. Holly, in particular, was once prized as a decoration for doors, windows, and mantels, because not only was it alive and green but it also snagged evil spirits before they could enter the house.

December 26

Look for a paraselene, or moon dog, whenever you see high, thin cirrus clouds near the moon. Moon dogs are saucers of reflected moonlight hovering to the side, sometimes attached to a halo. The sunlight version is a parhelion, or sun dog.

December 27

If you're up north, you might be lucky enough to see **auroras**, which occur when solar wind particles excite atoms in the upper atmosphere. It is the oxygen in the atmosphere that shines green, while the nitrogen contributes blues and reds.

The Inuits attributed auroras to the spirits of the dead playing soccer with walrus heads.

December 28

Is your soil naked? Keeping your soil covered with a layer of leaves or straw during winter protects plants and prevents excessive spring run-off. You'll be able to plant earlier next spring, too. Evergreen limbs are also good protection. Berry bushes—the Deadheads of the garden—particularly like the acid found in evergreen needles, so put that Christmas tree to good post-holiday use.

December 29

Foxes & Coyotes

In winter, foxes and coyotes hunt rodents by sound. After zeroing in on the ultrasonic squeaks, they pounce, crashing down into the snow with their front paws. This collapses the rodent's tunnel and neatly traps it.

December 30

As a winter storm approaches, you'll see this progression of clouds: high, thin, wispy cirrus clouds; fish scale–looking altocumulus; a lower layer of altostratus; and finally, dark nimbostratus.

December 31

Deep peace of the quiet earth to you
Deep peace of the shining stars to you
Deep peace of the shades of night to you
Moon and stars ever giving light to you

—Traditional Gaelic Blessing

Diane Olson is a writer who would

really like to get paid for crawling around in the dirt and watching bugs all day. A senior copywriter at McCann Worldgroup and former staff writer for *Catalyst* magazine, she has received nine awards for Excellence in Journalism from the Utah Chapter of the Society of Professional Journalists, and a Best of Utah from City Weekly for "Best Earth Mother."

Her "Urban Almanac" column, upon which this book is based, has been running in *Catalyst* for sixteen years. She has also written for *New York Spirit, Salt Lake Magazine,* and *Utah Homes and Gardens.* This is her first book.

Adele Flail is an artist, writer, and rogue biol-

ogist. Most recently working as the Science Gallery Coordinator for The Leonardo, Salt Lake City's sci + tech + art museum, her previous gigs have included everything from freelance graphic designer to clinical genetics tech, and she can now add book illustrator to her list. She lives on a nascent urban homestead with a dog, a cat, seven chickens, and a fiancé.